A BRIEF HISTORY

OF

CHRISTIAN WORSHIP

A Brief History
of
Christian Worship

James F. White

ABINGDON PRESS
Nashville

A BRIEF HISTORY OF CHRISTIAN WORSHIP

Copyright © 1993 by Abingdon Press.

Library of Congress Cataloging-in-Publication Data

White, James F.–
 A brief history of Christian worship. / James F. White.
   p. cm.
 Includes bibliographical references and index.
 ISBN 0-687-03414-0
 1. Public worship—History. 2. Liturgics—History 3. North America—Religious life and customs I. Title.
 BV5.W47 1993   92-32183
 264'.009—dc20   CIP

05 06 07 08 09 10 11 12—24 23 22 21 20 19 18 17 16 15

Printed in the United States of America on recycled, acid-free paper
Scripture quotations are from *The Holy Bible: New Revised Standard Version,* copyright 1989, Division of Christian Education of the National Council of the Churches of Christ in the United States of America. Used by permission.

In Memory of
and Gratitude for
My Three Great Teachers of Liturgy

Massey H. Shepherd, Jr.
(1913–1990)

Cyril C. Richardson
(1909–1976)

Edward Craddock Ratcliff
(1896–1967)

CONTENTS

PREFACE

The reader may well ask: "What need does the world have of yet another history of Christian worship?" It is a good question; there have been a number of general histories in the last half century. The works of Theodor Klauser and Herman Wegman were well enough thought of to be translated into English; Marion J. Hatchett, Richard M. Spielmann, and William H. Willimon have produced American volumes; and most of the English volume, *The Study of Liturgy*, and the French series, *The Church at Prayer*, consist of liturgical history. To these can be added countless other specialized historical studies.

Why add to their number? Our answer is largely in terms of perspectives. Each historian tells us almost as much about his or her own comfortable world as about the times and places they describe. The questions they ask, the sources they use, the approaches they take, each of these tells us about the world in which the author feels at home. None of the volumes we mention above were written in the 1990s with the possible exception of parts of the second edition of *The Study of Liturgy*. Most of them are foreign to American soil. They simply could not be expected to have the perspectives of a North American living in the last decade of the second millennium.

An important justification for the present work, then, is that it is written from the perspectives of the 1990s in North America. Those are its limitations as well as its advantages. But it is only natural that an American would ask questions that a European would not be likely to consider. One could not guess from reading Klauser or Wegman that anything of liturgical significance ever happened in North America. Wegman dismisses the three centuries before ours with the absolutely amazing statement that they were "the period of stagnation [in which] there was little positive contribution to the growth of Christian liturgy." These centuries receive fourteen out of his nearly four hundred pages of history.

If one reads the standard histories, one would never guess the contribution to liturgical history of such cultural phenomena as Jacksonian democracy, Enlightenment rationalism, or the fusion of worship and justice among English Quakers. These are of vital interest to us today in North America in order to understand ourselves.

But our perspectives will not be sufficient for others in the next decade or for Christians today in Africa. Other histories will be necessary with perspectives relevant to the needs of those times and places. Thus the writing of history is a humble procedure, at least when authors acknowledge the restraints of their own time and place.

What are those perspectives that distinguish this present work from its predecessors? One of our chief concerns is to recognize the cultural diversity inherent in Christian worship as in all human activities. Theologically this can be expressed as the witness of creation to what a lover of variety the Christian God appears to be. We are created in a variety of races, cultures, and with a multitude of languages. It is difficult, if not impossible, to make universal statements about human societies because the varieties are so infinite.

Variety also applies to such a worldwide phenomenon as the Christian worship of God. We can only indicate the vastness of variety in the Christian experience of worship while at the same time trying to trace the coherence that unites the various expressions in time and place. It is indeed high tribute to Christian worship that it can be expressed in such an infinite variety of forms as to be adapted to countless cultures ranging over two millennia in time and worldwide in space.

We shall try to take seriously the fact that North America, with its mixture of peoples, has been an immense liturgical laboratory. This is of major importance because in recent years so much of North American liturgical experiences has been exported by missionaries to Latin America, Africa, and Asia. But the liturgical experiences of North American Christians deserve a recognition they have rarely found in liturgical histories.

The most exciting sector of liturgical studies at present is the emergence of a North American school of liturgical history. At long last, dissertations and books are being written to explore North American experiences of Christian worship and what those experiences have to contribute to the rest of Christianity. I have had the privilege of working with many young scholars who are busy mapping out this previously unexplored terrain. Their findings are impressive: the liturgical creativity of the past two centuries in North America has hardly been equaled in any other period.

We must also take seriously the deep concern of all Christians for each other expressed in our time by the ecumenical movement. This means that the worship experiences of other traditions must be accorded respect and we must seek to understand others in order to know ourselves better. I long ago learned from Professor Cyril Richardson never to say anything negative about anyone's worship. As long as it survived, it obviously fulfilled some useful purpose in helping people glorify God.

At the same time, we must express concern that ecumenism has sometimes tended to stress consensus as if narrowing our possibilities were more important than expanding them. This seems to be a retrogressive attitude and is definitely not the approach taken in this present work. If the Creator seems to relish variety, perhaps we creatures should accept this in liturgy and maybe even in ethics. Our perspective here will be to affirm variety. We speak of "churches" throughout the book, rather than one standard uniform "church."

Our pace will be rapid, so detailed analysis is impossible. Frequently, whole books are compressed into a single sentence;

hardly any subject gets more than three paragraphs. The works listed in the bibliography should help one move further into the field. Our chief aim is to be balanced and comprehensive, which allows no space for details, however fascinating.

It remains to acknowledge how much I have learned in my ten years of teaching at the University of Notre Dame from my colleagues and students in the Graduate Program in Liturgical Studies. Grant Sperry-White and John Brooks-Leonard have kindly read chapters and contributed of their expertise to improve them. I appreciate the skills of Nancy Kegler, Sherry Reichold, and Cheryl Reed in making sense of my manuscript and producing a clean copy with such speed. Especially do I thank Mark Torgerson for his skill and diligence in tracking down elusive sources and data.

University of Notre Dame
May 7, 1992
J.F.W.

Worship in the Churches of the New Testament Era

The foundations for all subsequent Christian worship were laid in the decades in which the New Testament books were being written and edited, roughly the century following the resurrection of Jesus Christ. Every period of renewal since then has aspired to reach back to the principles and practices of the first Christian century; most debates about Christian worship have argued over the biblical evidence. The churches of the apostles and their immediate heirs have an authority for the Christian imagination that no other period can match. Golden age or not (I Cor. 11:29), all things liturgical are still tested by the standard of the earliest worshiping Christian communities.

This is the period when the canonical books of the New Testament were being written although no one recognized them as such at the time. But other sources from this period also fix our attention: the *Didache*, probably written in Syria late in the first century or early second; the so-called *Clement's First Letter*, most likely written in Rome in the last decade of the first century, and the letters of the martyred bishop, Ignatius of Antioch, from about A.D. 115. Even pagans contribute details to our knowledge such as a letter of Pliny, Roman governor of Bithynia about A.D. 112. So we are not destitute of information; the problem is how to evaluate what we can know about the worship of these Christian communities scattered from Jerusalem to Rome.

Our method will be to glimpse briefly the world the first Christians inhabited and the social realities they experienced. Who were these first Christians? Then we shall move on to see how they signified becoming Christian. How did they effect and experience this new order of being one in Christ? Then we examine what it was like living and dying as a Christian. How did they pray, give thanks, mark time, and support each other through life's crisis points? After that, we shall ask about the life of the Christian community itself in this period. How did it organize itself for ministry, preach the gospel, and use space and music? We must beware in this first century of presuming to know more than can be known from actual evidence. In other periods, the information becomes more voluminous, if not more comprehensible, and we shall follow approximately the same procedure.

THE WORLD OF THE FIRST CHRISTIANS

The primary liturgical document in any period is the worshiping community itself. So it is appropriate that we take a quick look at the people we encounter in the pages of the New Testament. Recent scholarship has taught us much about these early worshiping communities. For the most part, they are not the people we encounter in the pages of the gospels, chiefly village people of rural parts of Palestine, but people immersed in the urban centers of the Greco-Roman world. This much more cosmopolitan world had replaced the homogeneity of the village environment with urban life in cities crammed full of a variety of races, religions, and languages. Paul could readily find a Jewish community in most cities as he did in Antioch in Pisidia (Acts 13:14) or Thessalonica (Acts 17:1-2). Jews comprised about one seventh of the population of most Mediterranean cities.

Within these urban areas, the new converts to Christianity reflected a wide variety of social and educational levels.[1] Onesimus, the runaway slave, and Philemon, his wealthy owner, are social extremes but fellow Christians. And every level in between

14

seems encompassed among these early worshipers: Lydia the independent businesswoman dealing in luxury goods (Acts 16:14); Crispus, formerly ruler of the synagogue in Corinth (Acts 18:8); Dionysius, one of the governing council in Athens (Acts 17:34); and Cornelius, a Roman centurion (Acts 10:22), about as wide an assortment of "all sorts and conditions" as one could find in any society. Social stratification caused many of the problems in the churches, not least of all in the eucharist as at Corinth (I Cor. 11:20-22). Over against these social discrepancies Paul finds it necessary to assert the equality of baptism that transcends all human distinctions (I Cor. 12:13; Gal. 3:28; Col. 3:11).

The new Christian communities were only one tiny group within a vast assortment of clubs, associations, and religious bodies. Yet these Christian groups signaled membership in a radically new body by means of baptism which "signaled for Pauline converts an extra-ordinarily thoroughgoing resocialization, in which the sect was intended to become virtually the primary group for its members, supplanting all other loyalties."[2] And it was loyalty not just to a local church but to a new Israel which, like old Israel, transcended localities and nations. Apostolic visits and epistles, even pseudonymous ones, kept reminding them of this fact. We shall shortly be examining some of the worship patterns they held in common; there were also common structures of oversight and concurrence in belief patterns.

Many of these were inherited from Judaism, especially the ethical dimensions. Yet the old maps with which Judaism had plotted acceptable behavior no longer held firm for Christians. The accusation that Christians were "people who have been turning the world upside down" (Acts 17:6) was perceptive from the standpoint of Jewish tradition. Christians had adopted new definitions of what was pure and impure, new boundaries between what behavior was encouraged and what forbidden. Jerome Neyrey shows how Jesus had transformed the whole map of persons and places for meals. "Nothing, then, seems right according to the cultural rules for meals: no concern whatsoever is had for who is eating with whom, where, how or what is eaten. . . . Jesus' table-fellowship turns the world upside down for he welcomes anyone, especially sinners and the unclean, to eat with him anywhere and at anytime."[3]

But we must beware of overemphasizing the contrasts when it comes to worship. It is fundamental that Jesus was a Jew as were his earliest followers. A whole gamut of Jewish concepts and practices underlies Christian worship to this day. The concept that the saving power of a past event is brought into the present through reenactment is basic whether one is celebrating Passover or Good Friday. The recovering of past events through the observance of commemorative time underlies what both Christians and Jews still do. The experience of God's self-giving through ritual acts is a permanent part of Christian sacraments just as it is in Jewish worship. We cannot tell precisely how the Jewish understanding of the way to give thanks taught Christians to do so except that early eucharistic prayers show Christians learned the lesson well from Judaism. And even where early Christians might have found mentors in the pagan world, as in concepts of sacrifice, they preferred only Jewish teachers (Heb. 9:11-14). Christians may have turned the world upside down but in the form and content of their worship it was still recognizably a Jewish world.

BECOMING CHRISTIAN

We begin by looking at how the early churches signified the making of a Christian. There seems to be unanimity in this period in the practice of baptism as the means of identifying converts and including them within the Christian community. But details beyond the central act of a water bath are often indistinct.

Baptism had high authority in that the Lord himself had submitted to it at the beginning of his public ministry. All four gospels attest to this although not without some embarrassment (Matthew 3:15) since Jesus was sinless. For John the Baptist was preaching a baptism of repentance in the context of the last times. Some of John's converts were still around twenty years later (Acts 18:25; 19:1-7) but by then Christian communities had experienced a new reality of baptism, the activity of the Holy Spirit. In different ways but with similar effect, all four gospels portray Jesus' baptism

16

as a theophany of the Holy Spirit. Matthew expresses this as a promise: "He will baptize you with the Holy Spirit and fire" (Matt. 3:11).

The early churches were engaged primarily in a missionary undertaking so it is not strange that baptism is the best documented rite in the New Testament. According to John, Jesus' disciples began baptizing shortly after his baptism (John 4:2). Jesus equated baptism with his death (Mark 10:38; Luke 12:50) and this combination of baptismal and burial images became a perennial theme, still reflected in baptism today.

Baptism becomes the response expected from apostolic preaching. Pentecost may be the most dramatic instance: "Peter said to them, 'Repent, and be baptized every one of you'. . . . So those who welcomed his message were baptized, and that day about three thousand persons were added" (Acts 2:38, 41). The pattern is familiar: the word is preached, hearers become believers, they repent, and then are baptized. Making disciples leads to baptizing them.

All of this is done with urgency for they live at the edge of time and are prepared to enter a new age. Christian sacraments all have a strong eschatological flavor. Even marriage is a foretaste of the Kingdom, symbolized in Orthodox churches by the act of crowning the couple, as rulers of a new kingdom, the family. Baptism may be the most eschatological of all; it introduces one into a new community where the first fruits of the Kingdom are found. One rises from the watery grave of baptism in a new body, the Church, where the Holy Spirit dwells. One lives born again, having been cleansed of sin in passing through the waters. Baptism is initiation into God's new Kingdom of which the Church is a colony on earth. The eucharist is a lifelong renewal of baptism's initial foretaste of God's Kingdom.

The New Testament gives fascinating hints about the form and practice of baptism but we must not speculate beyond the actual evidence. It is tempting to take what we know from subsequent sources and read it back into this earliest period, but that produces more speculation than fact. But we can garner some information about the candidates, the actual practice, the formula

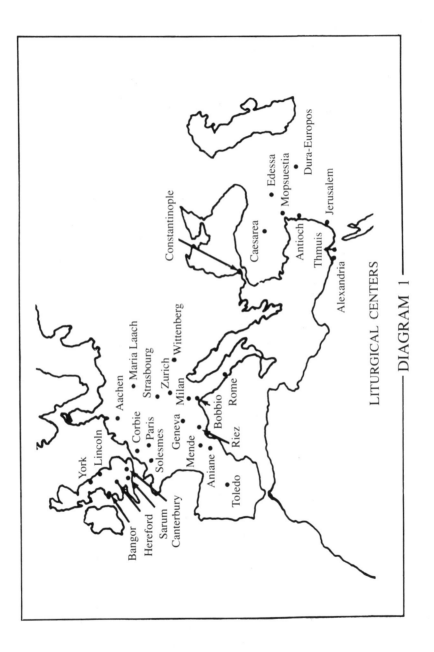

LITURGICAL CENTERS

DIAGRAM 1

used, the material, and attendant ceremonies. And we have even more evidence on how the act itself was interpreted.

The most vexing question, of course, is the age of candidates. Were they only adults, capable of professing faith themselves, or were families including small children also baptized? There is no direct evidence either for or against the baptism of infants in the New Testament churches. Those who are disinclined to baptize infants cite passages such as Mark 16:16 "The one who believes and is baptized will be saved" or Acts 2:38 "Repent, and be baptized." But those who baptize infants counter with the four household (*oikos*) passages which speak of the baptism of households: I Cor. 1:16 (Stephanas), Acts 16:15 (Lydia), Acts 16:33 (Philippian jailer), and Acts 18:8 (Crispus of Corinth). All of these speak of baptisms of "households," a term which included slaves and clients as well as immediate family.

Our most detailed account of a baptism occurs in Acts 8:35-39, the account of Philip and the Ethiopian eunuch. There is instruction, a request for baptism which contains the intriguing word "What is to *prevent* (*kolúei*) me from being baptized?", a question and answer as to belief (missing in some early texts), descent into water, Philip baptizes him, and they come up out of the water. It is intriguing for it tells us so much and so little. But the same sequence is still followed in adult baptisms: candidates are examined as to ethical and creedal commitment before being baptized.

The earliest baptismal formula seems to be baptism "in the name of the Lord Jesus" (Acts 19:5). This is corroborated by passages such as Acts 2:38 "in the name of Jesus Christ," "in the name of the Lord Jesus" (Acts 8:16), "calling on his name" (Acts 22:16), and Paul's rhetorical question "Or were you baptized in the name of Paul?" (I Cor. 1:13). In the first century, this formula was probably replaced by the familiar Trinitarian one found in Matthew 28:19, "in the name of the Father and of the Son and of the Holy Spirit." The same language is echoed in exactly the same words in the *Didache* (7). Ever since, virtually all the churches have followed this pattern although the United Pentecostal Church, International insists on the earlier "Jesus only" formula.

The *Didache* gives us more details as to the water. Running water is preferable, cold water is desired, but lacking these, "pour water on the head three times" (*Didache*, 7). This suggests that if the rest of the body could not be covered, at least the head should be deluged. The earliest surviving baptismal pools (several centuries later) indicate that the adult candidate stood in water a couple of feet deep while it was poured over his or her head. In addition, baptism, the *Didache* tells us, is an occasion for fasting by both baptizer and candidates.

Other ceremonies might accompany baptism but no consistent pattern emerges in the biblical accounts. These might include the laying on of hands, which signified and effected the transmission of the Holy Spirit. But the Spirit resists our attempts to hold a stop watch on its appearance: at Caesarea it fell on converts before baptism (Acts 10:44 and 47) and Ananias lays hands on Paul at his conversion so he might "be filled with the Holy Spirit" and then he is baptized (Acts 9:17). At other times, its arrival is postponed until sometime after baptism as in Samaria (Acts 8:16). Or at Pentecost it seems to come with baptism (Acts 2:38). The unifying thread seems to be that, unlike the baptism of John, Christian baptism is Spirit-filled. Somehow this is usually manifested in connection with the laying on of hands (Acts 8:18 and 19:6). The same image appears less frequently as sealing "by putting his seal on us and giving us his Spirit in our hearts" (II Cor. 1:22).

Presumably, the usual minister of baptism was whoever was in charge of the local congregation. Paul goes out of his way in I Corinthians 1:14-17 to dissociate himself from doing much baptizing: "For Christ did not send me to baptize but to proclaim the gospel" (17). On other occasions, Paul (at Ephesus, Acts 19:5), Ananias, and Philip (probably the deacon), take up this work the disciples had begun (John 4:2).

Baptism was such a universal experience for new Christians that it provided a ready point of reference for Paul and others in interpreting Christianity to recent converts. A variety of baptismal metaphors appears in Paul's epistles and other New Testament books. We cannot exhaust the list here and some are relatively minor: naming the name of the Lord, sealing, putting on Christ (as a garment), and entering the royal priesthood. But the five most important metaphors give us keen insight into what it was presumed baptism meant for early Christians and are reflected in subsequent baptismal rites. All of these metaphors overlap although no systematic presentation of baptism appears in the first two Christian centuries.

Baptism brings *union to Christ*. This is stated most forcefully in Romans 6:3: "Do you not know that all of us who have been baptized into Christ Jesus were baptized into his death? Therefore we have been buried with him by baptism into death so that, just as Christ was raised from the dead by the glory of the Father, so we too might walk in newness of life." A similar thought appears in Colossians 2:12. The connection of baptism and death and resurrection becomes a permanent theme in baptism and is dramatized whenever immersion is used ("enough water to die in"). Note that this is union with Christ's person (death and resurrection) and work (priesthood). Thus through baptism all Christians become priests, forming "a royal priesthood" (I Pet. 2:9). This is the basis for the priesthood of all believers as well as the ordination of both women and men.

Closely related to this metaphor of union to Christ is that of *incorporation into his body, the Church*. Nowhere is this described in such detail as in I Corinthians 12. Verse 13 relates "For in the one Spirit we were all baptized into one body—Jews or Greeks, slaves or free—and we were all made to drink of one Spirit." A similar passage occurs in Galatians 3:28 adding "no longer male and female" and Colossians 3:11 specifies also neither "circumcised or uncircumcised, barbarian, Scythian." Some exegetes would like to believe that a possible baptismal formula exists in these passages although that seems to stretch the evidence. First Corinthians 12 stresses the relatedness of the body's parts and the variety of gifts given to its members for the common good. The whole chapter leads directly to Paul's eulogy of love in Chapter 13 as the greatest of spiritual gifts. All these gifts are given by the Spirit for use in the body where baptism places us.

And the *gift of the Holy Spirit* itself is one of the signs of initiation into the community where it dwells. The early memories tied to the Day of Pentecost the promise "Repent, and be baptized . . . and you will receive the gift of the Holy Spirit" (Acts 2:38). Even earlier memories linked this manifestation to the appearance of the Spirit at the baptism of the Lord. Elsewhere, the gift of the Spirit is spoken of as being illumined or enlightened (Heb. 6:4) and as sanctification (I Cor. 6:11). Life in the church is life in the Spirit-filled community.

At the same time, it is a community of holiness. Baptism is linked in the same breath with both the *forgiveness of sins* and reception of the Holy Spirit: "repent, and be baptized, . . . so that your sins may be forgiven; and you will receive the gift of the Holy Spirit" (Acts 2:38). It is the most obvious sign of the act of washing: Paul is told by Ananias: "Get up, be baptized, and have your sins washed away, calling on his name" (Acts 22:16). Outward washing and the inward cleansing of "a good conscience" are linked in both I Peter 3:21 and Hebrews 10:22.

And finally, initiation is imaged as *new birth*, the most feminine of metaphors. This connects with being incorporated into a new body, the Church. The classic mention is John 3:5: "No one can enter the kingdom of God without being born of water and Spirit." Likewise, Titus 3:5 speaks of the "water of rebirth and renewal by the Holy Spirit." In the background is Paul's image of our becoming a new creation in Christ Jesus. So here we come full circle; baptism is both death and resurrection and new birth. The waters of baptism are both tomb and womb.

While the New Testament holds these varied metaphors in tension, the churches throughout history have tended to emphasize one or more of them and neglect the rest. The medieval churches placed a premium on forgiveness of sins while the priestly image of union to Christ receded. Incorporation into the Church seemed to grasp Calvin's imagination more than the others. Current efforts try to recover the balance of the New Testament metaphors since baptism is many things, all of them too important to overlook.

Baptism eventually led to the Lord's table and the eucharist is the only part of initiation that is repeated. But since it is repeated throughout life, we shall treat it in the following section although it also is a rite of initiation.

LIVING AND DYING CHRISTIAN

Our information about the day-by-day living out of one's baptism in the New Testament churches is limited but we shall sketch out what it meant in terms of daily public prayer, the eucharist, Christian time, and pastoral rites.

Daily Public Prayer

The New Testament contains abundant references to Christians assembling for the observance of daily prayer: "All these were constantly devoting themselves to prayer" (Acts 1:14). At first, these meetings may have been in common with other Jews who observed a daily schedule of corporate prayer but soon the Christian community formed its own assemblies. Nevertheless, "even if Christians did cease to pray in common with other Jews at an early date, the pattern of their worship was undoubtedly very strongly influenced by the Jewish worship from which it sprang" although with distinctive Christian embellishments.[4] This pattern apparently included a regular daily schedule of prayer services although it is difficult to tell what it was exactly. The *Didache* instructs Christians to pray the Lord's Prayer three times a day. This suggests that a regular daily cycle of hours for prayer, either public or private, was in operation in some areas, probably morning, noon, and evening in addition to prayer during the night.

Much of the incentive to prayer was the eschatological fervor of early Christians and the need to watch and wait for Christ's return. As Paul advises: "The Lord is near. Do not worry about anything, but in everything by prayer and supplication with thanksgiving let your requests be known to God" (Phil. 4:5-6). To what degree such prayers were communal or individual is hard to determine, especially outside of Jerusalem. Prayer services which included reading from scripture and "psalms and hymns and spiritual songs" (Eph. 5:19 and Col. 3:16) seem to be indicated in some places.

Whether they prayed in private or in groups, the prime characteristic of Christians' prayer seems to be that it was voiced in the name of Jesus: "If in my name you ask me for anything, I will do it" (John 14:14). The contents seem to focus around thankful praise of God and supplication for further benefits. Ignatius instructs: "Keep on praying for others too, for there is a chance of their being converted and getting to God" (Ephesians, 10). Above all else, prayer was to be constant: "Pray without ceasing" (I Thess. 5:17) became the favorite theme for a vast variety of patterns of prayer throughout the history of the Church.

The Eucharist

The biblical sources are more generous with information about the Lord's Supper (I Cor. 11:20) or breaking of bread (Acts 2:46, 20:7). Paul discusses it in I Corinthians and the Synoptic Gospels all give accounts of the Last Supper. We see in these accounts of the institution of the meal that there is already a growing diversity in local churches. Even so conservative a scholar as Joachim Jeremias is of the opinion that the differences between the various accounts occurred because "liturgical usage has influenced the formulation of the accounts of the Lord's Supper in many ways."[5] In the New Testament itself, we already see an important characteristic of Christian worship: regional variances within substantial unity. Even the memories of the words of the Lord Himself appear in the slightly differing versions of local churches, and if we were certain about the locales in which the gospels were written we could identify those churches. Luke's account (22:14-20) is closest to that of Paul (I Cor. 11:23-26). Luke is alone in mentioning a cup of wine before the bread (as well as afterwards) although the *Didache* places a single cup first. Mark (14:22-25) and Matthew (26:26-29) are closely related. Jeremias asserts Mark provides "the oldest text" and that "we have every reason to conclude that the common core of the tradition of the account of the Lord's Supper—what Jesus said at the Last Supper— is preserved to us in an essentially reliable form."[6]

The Fourth Gospel is silent about the meal itself, possibly because of the desire to keep the words of institution secret. Some scholars argued that John 6 provides parallels to the synoptic institution narrations. John also differs in dating the Last Supper on the day before the Passover meal while the Synoptics concur that it was the Passover feast. Indications of the Passover meal survive in the words of interpretation over the bread and cup, the eschatological nature of the event "until the kingdom of God comes" (Luke 22:18), the singing of a hymn (Mark 14:26), the reclining at table, the use of red wine, and the time and locale of the meal. On the other hand, no mention is made of the bitter herbs or the main entrée, roast lamb, nor is the usual word for unleavened bread used. Given John's propensity to symbolism and the desire to correlate the death of Jesus and the slaughter of lambs in the Temple on the afternoon before the Passover meal, the Johannine dating seems less reliable to this author, although many scholars do affirm John's chronology. In any case, the Last Supper occurs in the context of the Passover with its strong strain of recalling God's past work for God's people and fervent hope for the coming of the Messiah at the Passover. So clear was this identity that a group known as the Quartodecimans attempted to preserve the celebration of Easter on the Jewish Passover whether it came on a Sunday or not, and this movement lasted until the fifth century in parts of Asia Minor.

The Fourth Gospel also sets the meal in the context of an enacted parable, the footwashing (John 13:4-11). This survived in various churches such as Milan, where Ambrose in about 390 A.D. describes it (somewhat defensively) as part of the initiation ceremonies. Among the Milanese and Gallican churches it was retained as part of the Easter process of initiation. Some Anabaptist groups, especially Mennonites, revived it in the sixteenth century to accompany the Lord's Supper and Brethren groups did likewise in the eighteenth century. In modern times, footwashing has become part of Maundy Thursday observances in many churches.

What can we tell of the celebration of the Lord's Supper in the New Testament churches? Apparently it was long celebrated in the context of a meal. That this was not without problems is dramatically shown in the case of the Corinthian church where "one goes hungry and another becomes drunk" (I Cor. 11:21). Paul's solution is not to terminate the meal but to urge "if you are hungry, eat at home" (11:34). The meal did become detached, apparently in late New Testament times, for Jude 12 condemns those who "are blemishes on your love-feasts, while they feast with you without fear." By the beginning of the second century, the agape or love feast seems to have become a Sunday evening meal, at least in Bithynia, where in about 112 A.D. Pliny tells us Christians were willing to give up the meeting for "ordinary and harmless food" under persecution although unwilling to relinquish their early morning assembly presumably for the eucharist. Some argue that the prayers in *Didache* 9–10 relate to an agape meal rather than a eucharist but it may be a eucharist still including a meal: "after you have finished your meal, say grace" (10).

The proper conduct of the agape is prescribed in detail in the *Apostolic Tradition* in the early third century but the practice largely died out in western churches in the fourth century. It was revived by Moravians in the eighteenth century and given a new lease on life by John Wesley.[7] In recent years, it has had some popularity as an ecumenical alternative to the eucharist.

The frequency of the Lord's Supper in the first century is difficult to determine. Acts 2:46 speaks of the Jerusalem church: "Day by day, as they spent much time together in the temple, they broke bread at home and ate their food with glad and generous hearts, praising God." But even if this reference were to a daily eucharist it would be exceptional and could not have survived after the destruction of Jerusalem in 70 A.D. We have a hint of a Sunday observance in Acts 20:7 "On the first day of the week, when we met to break bread" and Pliny's letter of ca. 112 speaks "that on an appointed day they had been accustomed to meet before daybreak" for what certainly sounds like the eucharist. It is tempting to read backward from about 155 A.D. in Rome where Justin Martyr describes the eucharist as occurring "on the day called Sunday." A weekly celebration would seem to have been most likely in many New Testament churches.

The actual form the eucharist took is even harder to determine. There is every likelihood that, in a church predominantly Jewish in its first decades, Jewish forms of praying were most widespread and the evidence of later periods show them still surviving. Traces of the Jewish table prayer, *Birkat Ha-Mazon*, seem to be hinted at in the prayers of *Didache* 9–10. In both chapters, we see a bipartite structure of two thanksgivings and doxologies followed by a supplication.[8] The structures of both chapters are parallel as indicated with the operative words:

Ch. 9:

We thank you, our Father, for. . . . To you be glory forever.
We thank you, our Father, for. . . . To you be glory forever . . .
let your Church be brought together. . . . For yours is the glory and the power through Jesus Christ forever.

Ch. 10:

We thank you, holy Father, for. . . . To you be glory forever . . .
we thank you that you are mighty. To you be glory forever.
Remember, Lord, your Church, to save it. . . . For yours is the power and the glory forever.[9]

The *Didache* also says "In the case of prophets, however, you should let them give thanks in their own way." This acknowledges the existence of alternative patterns.

Soon a single pattern with many possible expressions of it firmly lodged itself in the Christian consciousness of how to give thanks in the eucharist. God is thanked for what God has done and then God is invoked to do still more, both present and future. Past, present, and future thus are gathered up in this form of prayer. This pattern of thanksgiving and supplication seems already to be in place by the end of the New Testament period and simply continues to be elaborated in future eras. Essentially Judaism had taught Christianity the form of prayer if not all its contents. Recent reforms have recovered this pattern in many churches.

When the *Didache* remarks: "in the case of prophets," we have an indication that there were still exceptional individuals with special gifts who could supersede the regular presider at the eucharist. But the usual presider seems to be the bishop or presbyter, terms sometimes used synonymously. At the end of the first century, *Clement's First Letter* advises: "For we shall be guilty of no slight sin if we eject from the episcopate men who have offered the sacrifices with innocence and holiness. Happy, indeed, are those presbyters who have already passed on."[10] Thus early on a predisposition for order seems apparent, summed up in Paul's phrase: "Let all things be done for building up" (I Cor. 14:26).

Emphasis on the community itself is even stronger. The eucharist not only binds them together but also excludes them from compromise with evil. A strong ethical dimension to the eucharist emerges early. As Paul writes to the Corinthians: "I do not want you to be partners with demons. You cannot drink the cup of the Lord and the cup of demons. You cannot partake of the table of the Lord and the table of demons" (I Cor. 10:21-22). Being in the eucharistic community demands making no concessions to evil. Participation in the eucharist excludes involvement in social evils both then and now. The eucharist is highly exclusive in the demands it puts on participants.

When we come to deciphering the meaning of the eucharist for New Testament Christians, we find a whole range of interpretations hinted at in the literature. No single mode of understanding comprehends the whole, yet all the parts fit together. It is important to gain a balance in order to avoid the one-sided interpretations of the eucharist that have so often clouded subsequent periods by their focus on a single item of meaning.

The very name eucharist suggests the *giving of thanks* and this is a central dimension, inherited from Judaism which characteristically approached God with thankful recital of God's acts. The *Didache* discusses the eucharist by explaining "how to give thanks." By the time of Ignatius (ca. 115 A.D.), the term "eucharist" is common enough for him to use it throughout his letters. The sense of thanksgiving is a joyful one resounding in "glad and generous hearts, praising God" (Acts 2:46-47) unlike the gloom with which later generations surrounded the eucharist.

The thanksgiving is given in *commemoration* of what God has already done. In both Luke and Paul's accounts of the institution the word *anámnesis* occurs. It is exasperatingly difficult to translate yet the significance is that of making present again something now past. "In remembrance of me" or recalling just does not capture the intensity of standing in the presence of what God has already done and experiencing anew its saving power. In recent years, we have come to realize that far more is commemorated than just the passion, death, and resurrection. Commemoration

28

begins with creation, a fact on which Jewish prayers seem quite clear. And it sweeps on through all the works of God until final consummation.

Another aspect is the intense level of *communion* among those who participate in the bread and cup. Paul asks: "The bread that we break, is it not a sharing in the body of Christ?" (I Cor. 10:16). And the *Didache* reminds us it is a community that is reconciled to each other, echoing the warning in the Sermon on the Mount about making an offering without being reconciled to one's brother or sister (Matt. 5:23-24). For Ignatius, the eucharist is a sure sign of unity: "For there is one flesh of our Lord, Jesus Christ, and one cup of his blood that makes us one, and one altar, just as there is one bishop along with the presbyters and the deacons."[11]

The New Testament has no explicit reference to the eucharist as *sacrifice* but the book of Hebrews makes frequent reference to Christ's work as sacrificial. Early Christians saw in the last of the Hebrew scriptures, Malachi, a reference to the eucharist: "in every place incense is offered to my name, and a pure offering; for my name is great among the nations" (1:11). The *Didache* latches on to this as a reference to the eucharist (14) and *Clement's First Letter* speaks in several instances of sacrifices and offerings (40 and 44) while referring to the eucharist. Since Christ was identified with the sacrificial lamb of God (John 1:29) these images eventually came to be applied to his presence in the eucharist.

And the *presence* of Christ was at the core of all these other images. For it was in the gathered community that he became known to them in the breaking of bread. The language of the institution narratives clearly identifies the bread with his body and the cup with the new covenant in his blood. Debate still rages over whether John 6:51-58 is a eucharistic passage but one can certainly read as eucharistic: "for my flesh is true food and my blood is true drink. Those who eat my flesh and drink my blood abide in me, and I in them" (55-56). Ignatius can refer to the eucharist in unmitigated terms as "the medicine of immortality, and the anti-dote which wards off death but yields continuous life in union with Jesus Christ."[12]

The presence of Christ is experienced through the *working of the Holy Spirit* although this is never explicit. Some exegetes read the baptismal passage, I Corinthians 12:13, with its conclusion "were all made to drink of one Spirit" as a eucharistic passage. But it was left to later centuries to state the work of the Holy Spirit in the eucharist more fully.

And finally, the eucharist is always on the edge of time, *looking to the eschaton* by proclaiming "the Lord's death until he comes" (I Cor. 11:26). It is a foretaste of the final culmination of things when Christ's beloved will feast with him in his heavenly banquet. It sums up all God's previous work (commemoration) and thrusts us onwards to what follows creation and redemption in the final consummation. It not only helps us envision what lies ahead but helps us already participate in it in a limited way.[13]

Christian Time

The Christian life also brought new concepts of time to the lives of early believers. We cannot find in the New Testament much development of the four cycles of liturgical time: daily, weekly, yearly, and lifetime. But there are hints of the planting of seeds from which each of these cycles would later sprout.

Already we have seen the tendency to seek out a daily schedule for prayer whether in individual or corporate form. Psalm 55 had mentioned three daily hours of prayer: "Evening and morning and at noon" (17), a number echoed in Daniel 6:10. There were other models in the Psalms such as "seven times a day I praise you" (119:164) in addition to "at midnight I rise to praise you" (119:62). Acts chronicles events at specific hours: Pentecost at "nine o'clock in the morning" (2:15); "About noon . . . Peter went up on the roof to pray" (10:9); "Peter and John were going up to the temple at the hour of prayer, at three o'clock in the afternoon" (3:1); and "About midnight Paul and Silas were praying and singing hymns to God" (16:25). These notations were to affect future developments. Jewish habits no doubt continued to set a daily rhythm of prayer for New Testament Christians but details are elusive.

Not much more definite is the weekly cycle which seems to focus on Sunday. The resurrection occurred at early dawn on the first day of the week and this day became the climax of the Christian week. At Troas "on the first day of the week, when we met to break bread" (Acts 20:7) suggests an early link of the eucharist to Sunday. Paul reminds the Corinthians as he had the churches of Galatia: "On the first day of every week, each of you is to put aside and save whatever extra you can" (I Cor. 16:2). And the Revelation of John specifies that John "was in the Spirit on the Lord's day" (Rev. 1:10).

The non-canonical literature tells us more. The *Didache* instructs "On every Lord's Day—his special day—come together and break bread and give thanks" (14). Ignatius notes that Christians "ceased to keep the Sabbath and lived by the Lord's Day, on which our life as well as theirs shone forth, thanks to Him and his death."[14] And Pliny asserts of Christians that "on an appointed day they had been accustomed to meet before daybreak."

In addition, the *Didache* deliberately avoids the Jewish fast days of Mondays and Thursdays and prescribes for Christians Wednesdays and Fridays for fasting (8). An influence from the Qumran Community may be present in this choice. Much later these days would be related to the events of Holy Week. So we see vague shadows of a developing weekly liturgical cycle with chief emphasis on Sunday.

The yearly cycle is much more sketchy although the scriptural accounts in the gospels and Acts were to be mined by later generations for raw material. It is faintly possible that I Corinthians 5:7-8 suggests a yearly Easter as a Christianized Passover: "Clean out the old yeast so that you may be a new batch, as you really are unleavened. For our paschal lamb, Christ, has been sacrificed. Therefore, let us celebrate the festival, not with the old yeast, the yeast of malice and evil, but with the unleavened bread of sincerity and truth." If so, it is a unique reference and the development of the yearly cycle comes later. The mention of Pentecost in I Corinthians 16:8 seems purely incidental.

Pastoral Rites

The lifetime cycle leads us to the pastoral rites, or occasional offices, or journeys and passages. Again, it is difficult to find much detail about these life-shaping events. As a general principle, the more marginal a person's relationship to the Christian community, the more important the pastoral offices become; for the lapsed Christian they may be his or her only contact with the community.

1. Reconciliation. First, as to journeys, i.e., events that are repeatable, we find scant information about reconciliation (penance) and healing. In general, the New Testament takes a hard line with baptized sinners. Paul threatens such a person in Corinth that "I will not be lenient" (II Cor. 13:2) and urges that a notorious sinner be handed "over to Satan for the destruction of the flesh" (I Cor. 5:5). Hebrews is just as pessimistic: "For it is impossible to restore again to repentance those who have once been enlightened, and have tasted the heavenly gift, and have shared in the Holy Spirit, and have tasted the goodness of the word of God and the powers of the age to come and then have fallen away, since on their own they are crucifying again the Son of God and are holding him up to contempt" (6:4-6). We are dealing, of course with major transgressions, such as apostasy, idolatry, and adultery. Only slowly is a process of reconciliation worked out for major sins.

2. Healing. Somewhat more hopeful is the parallel process of healing of bodily sicknesses. Jesus had performed many acts of healing and the apostles shared in this work: "They cast out many demons, and anointed with oil many who were sick and cured them" (Mark 6:13). Acts continues the chronicle of apostolic healing missions.

The classical description of healing is James 5:14-16. The sick are to "call for the elders of the church and have them pray over them, anointing them with oil in the name of the Lord. The prayer of faith will save the sick, and the Lord will raise them up; and anyone who has committed sins will be forgiven. Therefore confess your sins to one another, and pray for one another, so that you may be healed. The prayer of the righteous is powerful and effective." Prayer is clearly foremost, being mentioned four times in this brief passage but anointing with oil in the Lord's name also appears. Healing of the body and healing of the soul (confession) go hand in hand. And it is a corporate ministry in which not only the elders but the righteous take part. All Christians are to confess to one another and pray for one another.

3. Christian Marriage. We are at a loss to say much about marriage rites. The wedding feast at Cana (John 2:1-11) was Jewish, of course, and about all we know is that the wine flowed freely. From later evidence we know that Christians readily adopted many of the practices of both their Jewish and pagan neighbors, avoiding only the idolatry of the latter.

4. Christian Burial. We know even less about New Testament Christian burial rites. We can only assume that Jewish and pagan rites were again adapted minus any objectionable features. These events common to all peoples had well developed local customs that were not lightly discarded.

LIVING TOGETHER IN COMMUNITY

For the Christian communities to sustain life together, certain conventions soon became necessary. These include such matters as a variety of ministries, various methods for preaching the gospel, the use of music, and, eventually, the use of architecture. At this early stage, some of these were still in infancy, if born at all, but all led to substantial development in subsequent eras.

Leadership

One is struck by the variety of ministries that appears in the New Testament. All seem structured on a pragmatic basis: a need is apparent and a ministry to meet it develops. There is a need to distribute food so that the twelve can be free to devote themselves "to prayer and to serving the word" (Acts 6:4) and so the seven are chosen. Some fluidity is apparent, for Stephen certainly does not limit himself to the job description of waiting on tables. A common characteristic is that though there are varieties of services "to each is given the manifestation of the Spirit for the common good" (I Cor. 12:7).

The word "priest" is not used for any individual in the New Testament but the whole community has royal and priestly roles: "a royal priesthood" (I Pet. 2:9); "and made us to be a kingdom, priests serving his God and Father" (Rev. 1:6). A certain priority applies to the Twelve (Luke 6:13 and Rev. 21:14) and to other apostles such as Paul (Rom. 16:7; I Cor. 15:5, 7). But there are other gifts whose selection also comes from the Spirit: "God has appointed in the church first apostles, second prophets, third teachers; then deeds of power, then gifts of healing, forms of assistance, forms of leadership, various kinds of tongues" (I Cor. 12:28). All are activated by the same Spirit.

Certainly the most perplexing of these gifts, then and today, is that of tongues. It is not to be despised for it is a gift of the Spirit, one that Paul himself enjoyed (I Cor. 14:18), but clearly it is a headache. Glossolalia builds up the speakers but prophesy builds up the church. One is struck by the multiplicity of gifts which various members contribute to the worship life of the community: "when you come together, each one has a hymn, a lesson, a revelation, a tongue, or an interpretation." (I Cor. 14:26) But one criterion suffices for all these gifts: "Let all things be done for building up" (I Cor. 14:26). This implies intelligibility and that "all things should be done decently and in order" (I Cor. 14:40). In other words, a thoroughly pragmatic concern for the good of the *whole* community prevails.

Other leaders come about through human selection. It is tempting to draw parallels between the Jewish ruler of the synagogue (Acts 13:15) or the attendant (Luke 4:20) and Christian leaders but this is very risky business. There are numerous references to such offices as elders, presidents, teachers, overseers or bishops, and assistants or deacons. Their respective roles often seem to overlap and are difficult to distinguish. Frank Hawkins asserts that "scholars now generally agree that in the New Testament the terms *episkopos* [bishop] and *presbuteros* [elder] do not indicate two different levels of ministry. . . . In short, the threefold ministry of bishops, presbyters, and deacons cannot be convincingly traced back to the New Testament."[15] Clement's *First Letter* insists on a proper succession from the apostles either on a presbyteral or episcopal basis (42, 44). Ignatius is far more adamant: "Let the bishop preside in God's place, and the presbyters take the place of the apostolic council, and let the deacons (my special favorites) be entrusted with the ministry of Jesus Christ."[16] Power and control was increasingly being placed in the hands of fewer and fewer individuals.

Those chosen to lead the community might be recognized by various ritual acts besides election or appointment. In the case of the seven in Acts 6:6, the ritual act was laying on of hands with prayer by the apostles. This appears in other instances: Barnabas and Saul are set apart "after fasting and praying they laid their hands on them and sent them off" (Acts 13:3) or the recognition of an existing gift: "Do not neglect the gift that is in you, which was given to you through prophecy with the laying on of hands by the council of elders" (I Tim. 4:14) or again: "rekindle the gift of God that is within you through the laying on of many hands" (II Tim. 1:6).

The implication is that ministry stems from gifts and calling, both given by the Spirit. Some ministries may be formally recognized; others simply are exercized. The *Didache* gives the impression that prophets are basically above the rules but must be checked out to see if their calling is genuine. If they freeload off their hosts for three days or more they are obviously impostors (*Didache*, 11)! On the other hand, the community is told to "elect for yourselves bishops and deacons. . . . For their ministry to you is identical with that of the prophets and teachers" (*Didache*, 15). Clearly, the structure of ministerial leadership is still fluid but it is beginning to be set up in terms more familiar today.

Preaching

The ministry of preaching the word of God looms large as one of the chief responsibilities of the apostles and their assistants. The examples we have of sermons in the book of Acts are largely a proclamation of the work of Christ in the context of God's previous work for Israel. But these sermons (Acts 2:14-36; 3:12-26; 7:2-53; 13:16-41) are directed to Jews or to pagans (Acts 17:22-32) rather than to the Christian community. It is more difficult to decipher what kind of preaching went on among Christians. The synagogue service had certainly given precedents for preaching as a part of worship (Luke 4:16-30; Acts 13:14-16). It usually followed readings from the law and prophets and often was a commentary on them.

We have no clear evidence of an exactly similar process in Christian worship until the middle of the second century, but it is tempting to believe that it existed from an early time. We have a few elusive references: in Jerusalem after the release of Peter and John those in the community "were all filled with the Holy Spirit and spoke the word of God with boldness" (Acts 4:31). This suggests individual testimonies or some form of common witnessing.

There are some indications that Paul "reckoned on the reading of his letters in the service, . . . [in] the construction of most of them: it is so arranged that the reading aloud of the letters fits into the framework of a service, or in important sections takes its place (Formula of greeting, Introductory prayer, Statements of the theme of the preaching, Hymnic sections, Concluding prayer for grace, etc.)."[17] Revelation 1:3 presupposes a public reading, most likely in worship. It is less certain until the next century that the Hebrew scriptures were actually read in Christian worship.

Scholars have been intrigued by the possibility that the gospels may have been composed with the needs of a lectionary in mind. For a time it was a rather popular sport to find a lectionary inherent in the gospels although very difficult to prove. One scholar found the paschal vigil gave a structural basis for the book of Revelation. Eventually, of course, lectionaries did segment parts of the gospels for each Sunday but it seems unlikely that this was the organizing principle in the composition of these books.

Though we can speak about the likelihood of liturgical preaching, we can do little more than speculate. At Troas, in the context of the eucharist, Paul "continued speaking until midnight" (Acts 20:7) and put one of his hearers to sleep, a tradition still very much with us! But for most hearers, these sermons must have been a welcome proclamation of what God had done, is doing now, and promises yet to accomplish.

Church Music

We cannot be very definite with regard to music except to note the number of places that speak of the singing of hymns even in such uncomfortable places as the Philippian jail (Acts 16:25). The joy of Christian worship is reflected in singing: "as you sing psalms and hymns and spiritual songs among yourselves, singing and making melody to the Lord in your hearts" (Eph. 5:19; Col. 3:16).

Differentiating among these three items—psalms, hymns, and spiritual songs—is not easy for they all seem to focus on praise. Even pagans noticed that Christians sang "a hymn to Christ, as to a God" (Pliny).

The book of Revelation is especially prone to comment on singing as a feature of the heavenly Church and hence, we may presuppose, of the Church on earth. The seer speaks of "a new song" (5:9 and 14:3), in the first instance a Christological hymn. The singers hold a harp (Rev. 5:8; 15:2). Ignatius also uses the harp and its strings as a metaphor of the relationship of the presbyters to the bishop (Ephesians, 4). Objections to other instruments besides the lyre and harp arose because of associations with pagan worship but these two were associated with King David.[18] Likewise, objections to women singers which arose later on do not seem to have troubled the New Testament churches. Ignatius, who likes musical metaphors, says "harmonious love is a hymn to Jesus Christ" and suggests that "taking your pitch from God, you may sing in union and with one voice to the Father through Jesus Christ" (Ephesians, 4).[19]

We have glimpses of various hymn texts although these are impossible to identify with certainty. The Christological hymn in Philippians 2:6-11 is a most likely candidate as probably are Romans 11:33-35, Colossians 1:15-20, Ephesians 5:14, and possibly the hymn on love in I Corinthians 13. The first two chapters of Luke contain the hymns of Elizabeth (1:42-45), Mary (1:46-55), Zechariah (1:68-79) and Simeon (2:29-32). All of these combine the language of Jewish history and the personal experience of the singer. They readily lend themselves to corporate recital and have been so used for centuries. Revelation is full of songs: 4:11, 5:9-10; 11:17-18; 15:3-4.

To these hymnic fragments must be added a vast array of creedal phrases such as "Jesus is Lord" (I Cor. 12:3), greetings such as "Grace to you and peace from God our Father and the Lord Jesus Christ" (Gal. 1:3), doxologies (Rev. 1:4-6; Jude 24-25), and benedictions such as the concluding grace of II Corinthians 13:13, often called the "apostolic benediction" and still in contemporary use. To these may be added various exclamations such as "Come, Lord Jesus" (I Cor. 16:22; Rev. 22:20), the cry "Abba!

Father!" (Rom. 8:15), and the Jewish word of confirmation "Amen" (I Cor. 14:16).

Nor should we forget that gestures often speak louder than words. Especially prominent is the holy kiss (I Cor. 16:20) or kiss of peace. Mention is made of this in the synoptics, Paul's letters, I Peter, and in Acts. Certainly not all these are liturgical uses but some have argued that, serving as a closing to four of Paul's epistles, mention of the kiss suggests a liturgical rubric.[20] The peace becomes common in worship in later centuries and it is tempting to read it back into the first.

Church Architecture

As to the architectural setting of worship in the New Testament, it seems largely confined to private homes such as the third floor apartment in Troas (Acts 20:9). In several instances, such as that of Philemon, it was a private home (1:2). This indicates relatively small assemblies, often meeting behind locked gates (Acts 12:12-16), breaking bread at home (Acts 2:46). In Ephesus, Paul used a lecture hall for two years (Acts 19:9-10) although this does not necessarily indicate worship. The various references to baptisms suggest that some occurred in homes (Acts 10:47; 16:33) but on such occasions as Pentecost the three thousand must have been baptized in some outdoor pool.

FOR FURTHER READING

Beasley-Murray, G. R. *Baptism in the New Testament*. Exeter: Paternoster Press, 1962.

Bradshaw, Paul F. *The Search for the Origins of Christian Worship*. London: S.P.C.K., 1992.

Cullmann, Oscar. *Early Christian Worship*. London: S.C.M. Press, 1953.

Delling, Gerhard. *Worship in the New Testament*. Philadelphia: Westminster Press, 1962.

Delorme, J., et al. *The Eucharist in the New Testament*. Baltimore: Helicon Press, 1964.

George, A., et al. *Baptism in the New Testament*. Baltimore: Helicon Press, 1964.

Hahn, Ferdinand. *The Worship of the Early Church*. Philadelphia: Fortress Press, 1973.

Jeremias, Joachim. *The Eucharistic Words of Jesus*. New York: Charles Scribner's Sons, 1966.

Kilmartin, Edward. *The Eucharist in the Primitive Church*. Englewood Cliffs: Prentice-Hall, 1965.

Léon-Dufour, Xavier. *Sharing the Eucharistic Bread: The Witness of the New Testament*. New York: Paulist Press, 1987.

Marshall, I. Howard. *Last Supper and Lord's Supper*. Grand Rapids: Eerdmans Publishing Company, 1981.

Martin, Ralph P. *Worship in the Early Church*. London: Marshall, Morgan, and Scott, 1964.

Moule, C. F. D. *Worship in the New Testament*. London: Lutterworth Press, 1961.

Schnackenburg, Rudolf. *Baptism in the Thought of St. Paul*. Oxford: Basil Blackwell, 1964.

Worden, T., et al. *Sacraments in Scripture*. London: Geoffrey Chapman, 1966.

Worship in the Churches of the Early Christian Centuries

The five hundred years after the New Testament period saw enormous changes in every aspect of Christian worship. In this chapter, we shall examine those changes from about 133 A.D., the end of the period of scripture writing, until 604 A.D., the death of Pope Gregory I. In these five centuries, the outlines of worship sketched out in the New Testament period were filled in with great detail, providing many of the practices still current.

During this period, Christianity spread to encompass the entire Mediterranean world and the rest of the Roman Empire which covered Europe west of the Rhine and Danube. Christianity reached even beyond the empire in Ireland, Armenia, and Persia. This growth brought a wide variety of peoples of different cultures and languages to allegiance to Jesus Christ. All these peoples developed distinctive forms of worship, contributing their own cultural characteristics, yet preserving an essential unity. Tracing this unity in diversity is difficult because similar developments often came at different times in different places.

Fortunately for us, the sources from this period are much more abundant than in the New Testament era. They may be classified in a number of genres which include: church orders (on how to run a well-managed church), apologies (to convert pagans), catechetical lectures (for converts), theological and practical treatises, sermons, letters, rules (for monastic communities), collections of prayers, travel notes (from pilgrims), scriptural commentaries, histories, and the visual evidence (paintings, sculpture, and architectural remains).

This massive documentation still leaves many questions unanswered, resulting in major gaps in our information. For example, there is an almost complete lack of information from Rome itself for several centuries. And much of the data we do possess is subject to a wide range of possible interpretations. So we must not presume to know more than can be known about this period. This is particularly sensitive since so many of the materials from this epoch have been mined as ore for the reforms of the last third of the twentieth century. (The word "reform" throughout this study will be used in a value neutral sense as anything producing change whether for better or for worse. The use of the term in the titles of bills introduced into Congress illustrates this!)

One final caution; nothing stands still. Each of the items we shall examine continues to evolve throughout this period. We can only trace the general tendencies of development, or rather, those developments for which surviving documents give us some information.

THE WORLD OF THE EARLY CHRISTIAN CENTURIES

The social changes of this period read like a catalog of opposites. From small cells of devout folk meeting in secrecy to vast crowds of the populace worshiping in imperial basilicas, Christianity went within a century from being the object of persecution to the official religion of the empire. From a religion largely confined to the eastern fringe of the Mediterranean to one stretching from Ireland to Persia, the geographical scope multiplied many times. From a simple gospel message to a highly sophisticated theology, Christianity went from being virtually unknown to dominating the intellectual world of late antiquity.

But even the empire which it came to dominate proved to be far from stable. Under Constantine, it was divided into east and west. Neither portion was immune from barbarian attack and the unthinkable happened in 410: Rome fell. By 430, barbarians were attacking North Africa as Augustine lay dying in Hippo. Most of these invaders eventually became Christians themselves, adding even further to the cultural diversity of the Mediterranean basin. In the seventh century, Islam conquered the African ramparts of Christianity and many of its bastions in the east. North African Christianity all but disappeared and Christians south and east of the Mediterranean again became and have remained tiny isolated minorities.

Those Christians of the fourth century who had managed to survive the persecutions of the emperor Diocletian must have been amazed when, after the battle of the Milvian Bridge in 312, Constantine championed Christianity. No wonder he was welcomed as the equal of the apostles, a title hardly warranted by his morals! But he was indeed a generous benefactor, especially in terms of real estate. Imperial basilicas were turned over to Christians who once had entered such buildings to be tried as accused criminals. And large new basilican churches were built in Rome, Constantinople, Bethlehem, and Jerusalem.

Christianity became a legal religion in 313 and the official religion of the empire in 380. The changes for Christianity in our own times in the former Soviet Union are mild compared to those happening to fourth-century Christians. Suddenly their furtive assemblies had become public convocations. It was necessary to re-envision worship with a new sense of scale. Simple ceremonial was replaced with elaborate performances. Space always dictates what is possible and the house-church simplicity yielded to imperial magnificence in the new churches. Despite occasional periods and places of persecution, Christian worship has never since relinquished for long the appearances of an imperial religion.

The same shift is obvious in the organizational structure of the churches. The early rather ad hoc organization with a variety of ministries, ordained and charismatic, increasingly gave way to a standardized form imitating in many ways the grades and jurisdictions of the empire itself. The incipient hierarchical patterns we have seen suggested by Ignatius prevailed increasingly. Even so, the medieval practice of sequential ordination was as yet far off.

Ambrose was elected, baptized, and ordained bishop of Milan in 373; Nectarius became Patriarch of Constantinople in 381 by the same procedure. And many deacons, including Leo I and Gregory I, became bishops of Rome, never having been priests.

The tendency to move from freedom to formula developed within liturgy in various parts of the world.[1] In the mid-second century (ca. 155), Justin Martyr, a Roman lay person and teacher, in his *First Apology* tells us the president at the eucharist prays "to the best of his ability." About sixty years later, a church order, *The Apostolic Tradition*, (usually attributed to the Roman priest, Hippolytus) does prescribe the texts for prayers for ordinations, baptisms, and eucharists, but concedes "it is not at all necessary for him [the bishop] to utter the same words as we said above. . . . If indeed anyone has the ability to pray at length and with a solemn prayer, it is good. . . . Only, he must pray what is sound and orthodox."[2] But room for even this much spontaneity increasingly shrank. By the mid-fourth century, Sarapion, bishop of Thmuis in Egypt, was using a whole *euchologion* or collection of prayers which somehow has survived. We see a definite shift from a high degree of pastoral discretion in ordering worship and articulating prayer to formal fixity in invariable formulas and structures.

Obviously, many of these changes came about at different rates in different places. The era of worldwide liturgical standard-ization was far in the future. There is recognizable unity among the various churches in this period but great regional variety. This period gives abundant precedents for inculturation. Anscar J. Chupungco distinguishes between "the theological content [which] refers to the meaning of the rite, while the liturgical form refers to the ritual shape with which the content is visibly ex-pressed. The theological content is constant. . . . The liturgical form, on the other hand, has undergone and continues to un-dergo changes or modifications in the course of time because of prevailing theological and cultural factors."[3] Although we may be unconvinced about the historical witness to the constancy of theological content, there is certainly much truth about the rela-tive character of liturgical forms.

Already in the New Testament narratives we have seen slightly differing traditions as to the words spoken at the Last Supper. In the centuries that lay ahead, Christianity spread to all the cultures of western Europe, the Middle East, and northern Africa. Local ways of expressing oneself, customs of celebrating events (particularly rites of passage), fondly remembered local heroes of the faith (martyrs and other saints), local agricultural seasons, and familiar local traditions, all gave regional color to Christian worship as it developed. While documenting an essential unity, we must also acknowledge these local distinctions as an important ingredient in the history of Christian worship.

With this liturgical diversity early popes seemed to be in accord, at least in areas beyond their own immediate jurisdiction. Pope Gregory I sent Augustine of Canterbury to England about 596 with the advice: "Your brotherhood is familiar with the usage of the Roman Church since you have very pleasant memories of being raised and nurtured in that usage. But it seems to me that you should carefully select for the English Church, which is still new to the faith and developing as a distinct community, whatever can best please Almighty God, whether you discover it in the Roman Church, or among the Gauls, or anywhere else. For customs are not to be revered for their place of origin; rather those places are to be respected for the good customs they produce. From each individual church, therefore, choose whatever is holy, whatever is awe-inspiring, whatever is right; then arrange what you have collected as if in a little bouquet according to the English disposition and thus establish them as custom."[4] This liturgical laissez-faire has characterized Christian worship during three-fourths of its history.

BECOMING CHRISTIAN

The process of becoming a Christian underwent rapid development in the century immediately following the New Testament period. Although the process is still in flux even today, many practices had lodged themselves firmly in place by the beginning of the third century. Many recent reforms have been inspired by the various paradigms for Christian initiation that developed in this early period.

Justin Martyr wrote his *First Apology* about 155 A.D. He tells us that new Christians first are examined as to creedal and ethical commitment, then they "are brought by us where there is water, and are reborn by the same manner of rebirth by which we ourselves were reborn; for they are then washed in the water in the name of the Trinity."[5] "This washing," he tells us, "is called illumination." The newly baptized are then led to the assembled community where prayer is offered for them, they are greeted with a holy kiss, and initiation concludes with the eucharist. Since baptism is in the nude at this time, the washing is not public. But once baptized and reclothed, they are welcomed for the first time to the community's eucharist.

Other second century writers add interpretations. The *Shepherd of Hermas*, visions probably written in Rome, tells us that after baptism's "remission of our former sins" only "one repentance" is left. The reference is to major sins. Irenaeus of Lyons, in his treatise *Against the Heresies* (about 190), compares baptism to the moisture that makes flour into dough and bread. To our bodies, it gives "the unity which brings us to immortality"; to our souls, it conveys the Holy Spirit. For Clement of Alexandria in *The Tutor* (about 200) baptism means enlightenment, adoption, and being made perfect. As a washing, it cleanses from sin; as a gift of grace, it removes the penalties of sin; as an enlightenment, we are "made keen to see the divine"; and as perfection, nothing is lacking for "him who has the knowledge of God."

By the third century, our information expands enormously. From Tertullian in North Africa we have the first treatise on a sacrament, his *On Baptism* (about 200). *The Apostolic Tradition* (about 217) devotes several pages to detailing the whole process of initiation. Tertullian tells us water can convey sanctity when God is invoked and thus can cleanse both body and soul. After the washing, he tells us, we are anointed with oil, following the custom by which Moses anointed Aaron for priesthood and we receive the laying on of hands "inviting and welcoming the Holy Spirit." The minister of baptism is normally the bishop, presbyter, or deacon but "even laymen have the right: for that which is received on equal terms can be given on equal terms."[6]

He goes on to argue that the Passover (Easter) is the "day of most solemnity for baptism," as uniting us to the Lord's passion although any time during the great fifty days of Eastertide is appropriate because of the Lord's resurrection appearances and mission of the Holy Spirit. Beyond that, any time is suitable. Only let those who are to receive baptism prepare with prayer, fastings, confession, and all-night vigils.

The general pattern he describes in North Africa in a treatise, *Of the Crown* (ca. 211) is corroborated in detail by the *Apostolic Tradition*. Tertullian describes renunciation of the devil, questioning, triune immersion, welcome to the assembly, and reception of milk and honey (a sign of the promised land). *On Baptism* also clearly demonstrates beyond any doubt that, by the third century, children are being baptized, for Tertullian opposes this practice and even the baptism of the unmarried. The *Apostolic Tradition* also gives unmistakable evidence that children are being baptized, many of them still too young to "speak for themselves." From this point on, there is no doubt about the baptism of infants. Theological developments in the fourth century were to make it the normal practice everywhere for well over a millennium.

The *Apostolic Tradition* describes in detail the entire process of initiation as practiced in fourth-century Rome. First begins a period as hearers of the word during which inquiry is made as to their state of life and profession. This eliminates anyone compromised with pagan culture or engaged in unethical practices. The period as hearer of the word could last up to three years. Indeed, some converts might be martyred before their period of testing was over, and were considered to have been baptized in their own blood.

This long period, known as the catechumenate, involved a course of instruction and prayer, always apart from those already baptized, with whom catechumens were not allowed to pray, give the kiss of peace, nor receive communion. Each year, some of the catechumens were chosen for final preparation for baptism. (If all this sounds much like the contemporary Roman Catholic Rite of Christian Initiation of Adults in our times it is not accidental; the *Apostolic Tradition* was the chief source of the new rite.) Those chosen to receive baptism each year (the elect) underwent intensive preparation including further examination of life style and daily exorcisms. All this culminated in the final three days, which we presume came at Easter with fasting, praying, and exorcism.

At cockcrow on Easter morning, the candidates assemble at the font, renounce Satan, are anointed with oil of exorcism, undress, descend into the water, are examined as to belief (in words similar to what we call the Apostles' Creed), are immersed after each of the three divisions of the creed, are anointed with the oil of thanksgiving, dress, and enter the church. There the bishop lays hands on them, invoking God's grace, and then pouring oil of thanksgiving on their head. Some see the bishop's actions as simply the conclusion of baptism and not as a separate rite. The newly baptized then join with the faithful in prayer and give the kiss of peace for the first time. All then receive the eucharist. At this occasion, the initiates receive also a cup of water and a cup of milk and honey. Further instruction may follow in private. Later in the third century, the *Didascalia Apostolorum* (a church order most likely from Syria) points out the need for a woman deacon to baptize and anoint the female candidates (who are nude) and to teach them after baptism: "For this cause we say that the ministry of a woman deacon is especially needful and important. For our Lord and Saviour also was ministered unto by women."[7]

At least by the fourth century, initiation was firmly tied into the paschal celebration, baptism coinciding with the time and day of the resurrection. It came after a long period of preparation and training both ethical and creedal. And baptism with its anointings and laying on of hands always culminated in the eucharist. There was a unity in the rites of initiation regardless of the age of the recipient. The formulas used are Trinitarian and the *Apostolic Tradition* links the holy church to mention of the Holy Spirit. The number, sequence, and interpretations of the anointings varied from region to region. They often include the oil of exorcism applied over the entire naked body (symbolizing, for some writers, Adam in his state of innocence before the fall), and oil of thanksgiving applied to the head (Rome apparently having two such anointings). The connection between the words "anoint" and "Christ" would have been clear in Greek or Hebrew.

47

When Christianity became respectable under Constantine, major changes occurred. In this period, our documentation increases and from the fourth and fifth century we have architectural remains as well as the lectures bishops from Jerusalem to Milan gave in explaining to the newly baptized that which they had just received. Some of these mystagogical catecheses (lectures explaining the sacraments of initiation) give us a play by play account of what the new Christians had only recently experienced. They also provide some of the earliest interpretations of the various sacraments of initiation. In a sense, they are the beginnings of sacramental theology. Although not written in a systematic fashion, they interpret, often in allegorical terms, what the new Christians had just experienced.

Cyril, bishop of Jerusalem about 350 A.D. (or possibly his successor, John), begins his first post-baptismal catechesis: "Let us now teach you exactly about these things that ye may know the deep meaning to you-ward of what was done on that evening of your baptism."[8] He then relates the renunciation of the devil while facing West, the move to the baptistry, examination of faith in the Trinity, descent "three times into the water" as imitation of death and resurrection, and anointing, "the emblem of that wherewith Christ was anointed: and this is the holy Ghost." The whole concludes with a discussion of the eucharist.

A few decades later, far away in Milan, Ambrose tells the newly initiated of the *effeta* (Mark 7:32-35) or opening of ears and nostrils. As he delivers his lecture series to new Christians, he reminds them of the font whose shape resembled a tomb into which they were plunged and from which they had emerged. Ambrose points out that Milan has a custom of footwashing and, somewhat defensively asserts that "it is a sacrament and means of sanctification" even though the Roman Church has no such custom: "This I say, not to find fault with others, but to recommend my own usage . . . we too are not without discernment."[9] Until this day, the Archdiocese of Milan follows its own rites for the sacraments, deferring but not yielding to Rome. After the other portions of the rite comes the "spiritual seal" in which "at the invocation of the priest, the Holy Spirit is bestowed . . . [Isa. 11:2-3], as it were the seven virtues of the Spirit." At this time, this act is still an integral part of baptism; later theologians used Ambrose to argue that though the Spirit is given in baptism its gifts come in what was subsequently named confirmation.

Other practices and interpretations show up at about the same time in lectures John Chrysostom gave in Antioch (ca. 390). The renunciation is followed by the adhesion in which, having renounced the devil, the new Christian enters Christ's service with the words: "And I enter into thy service, O Christ." The one being baptized goes down into the water and apparently his or her head was then lowered beneath the water. A passive form of the baptismal formula is used: "'So-and-so is baptized in the name of the Father, and of the Son, and of the Holy Spirit,' he [the priest] puts your head down into the water three times and three times he lifts up again, preparing you by this mystic rite to receive the descent of the Spirit. For it is not only the priest who touches the head, but also the right hand of Christ, and this is shown by the very words of the one baptizing."[10] The passive form shows that the priest does not baptize (as implied by the western form "I baptize") but that he is only through whom baptism is effected. This understanding still distinguishes eastern churches from those of the West.

In still another location, catechetical lectures have survived of Theodore, Bishop of Mopsuestia in Asia Minor, delivered about 390. He tells us dramatically of exorcists praying for victory over Satan. Having disrobed, the candidates are anointed all over with holy Chrism, "a mark and a sign that you will be receiving the covering of immortality, which through baptism you are about to put on."[11] The priest invokes the Holy Spirit to impart power to the water both of "conceiving . . . and becoming a womb to the sacramental birth." After baptism, a white garment is placed on the new Christian and he or she is signed on the forehead by the priest with the words: "So-and-so is signed" in the name of the Trinity. Theodore traces this to the Holy Spirit at Jesus' baptism and Jesus' calling himself anointed (Luke 4:18).

What we have seen in these late fourth-century preachers is a rite still integrated that proceeds from opening exorcism through baptism, various anointings, laying on of hands or signing or sealing, and concludes with the eucharist. A fullness of sign is evident. Baptism is done in an abundance of water; usually baptism is compared to death and the operative verbs are "descend" or "plunge" and "ascend" or "go out." Images of the womb and Christ's baptism also occur. Care is exercised that those baptized, except for children, have a full period of instruction prior to baptism. Egeria, a Spanish woman who visited Jerusalem about 384 A.D., tells us of the bishop in Jerusalem that "during the forty days he goes through the whole Bible" and "after five weeks teaching they [the elect] receive the Creed." They are told "during the eight days of Easter after you have been baptized" baptism will be explained. "Then, the bishop expounds the mysteries and interprets them."[12]

We have seen both similarities and differences between local churches. Each seems to guard local practices with a certain pride in doing things the way they have always been remembered in that locale. But a major split began to become apparent by the early fifth century. As Christianity spread out from urban areas, bishops became less and less able to minister to country regions and presbyters undertook leadership of rural parishes. Italy, with an unusually large number of bishops, remained something of an anomaly.

Two types of conservatism developed with diametrically opposing results. The churches of the East and Egypt were determined to retain the unity of initiation and have done so to the present day by allowing a presbyter to anoint immediately after baptism with chrism already blessed by the bishop. Thus candidates, usually babies, are baptized, sealed, and communicated at one occasion. This unity has intrigued many churches of the West in recent years and some have endeavored to make initiation complete in one service at whatever age.

The West, though, sought to preserve the connection between initiation and the ministry of the bishop. Pope Innocent I wrote Bishop Decentius of Gubbio in 416: "As to the consignation of the newly baptized, clearly no one other than the bishop is permitted to perform it."[13] Even so, presbyters frequently also performed this function in Spain, Gaul, and probably in North Africa. Innocent's decree eventually became part of canon law and shaped western practice. Anglicans still follow it faithfully;

Roman Catholics have made important exceptions for adult baptisms and for the dying.

Unfortunately, there was a practical flaw in the western conservatism, namely the availability of bishops, especially as Christianity spread into the vast tribal dioceses of northern Europe. The principle of no bishop, no confirmation (as this function came to be called) was resolved on a practical basis, not a theological one. The consequence was a wrenching apart of the segments of initiation, once so happily united. But the full dissolution came later.

We have already seen that infants were certainly being baptized by the beginning of the third century, if not long before that. Various factors were to contribute to making infant baptism the normal practice in both East and West. Many adults, including Constantine himself, delayed baptism until their deathbed, thereby avoiding the need ever to become a penitent because they could erase all their sins at once. But this so-called clinical (bed) baptism was strongly discouraged because no one knows the date of their death. Most forceful was the teaching of Augustine of Hippo with regard to the connection of sin and baptism. Through baptism, he taught, "infants die to original sin only; adults, to all those sins which they have added, through their evil living, to the burden they brought with them at birth."[14] No one could risk dying with the guilt of original and actual sin although Augustine, who certainly had his share of the latter, was not baptized himself until age 32.

Augustine's influence on baptismal theology extended in another direction. In his battles with the Donatists (who insisted that only holy men could celebrate authentic sacraments), Augustine insisted that the source of sacraments is God, not the minister. Sacraments are not contingent on the moral character or even beliefs of the minister but receive their efficacy from God alone. The Donatists had rightful sacraments even though they held them unrightfully which interfered with their efficacy. Hence rebaptism, which had been advocated earlier in North Africa by Cyprian, could not be practiced. This is of enormous ecumenical significance in our times, for it means cross-denominational acceptance of each others' baptisms.

The essentials of initiation were similar: instruction, baptism, some sign of the Holy Spirit, and first communion. But the time sequence, the ministers of the portions, the types and number of accompanying ceremonies (anointings, footwashings, adhesion), differed according to what church one was in. And interpretations of these various acts differed even more. Local traditions were carried by missionaries as they won new areas for Christianity. Variety and unity remained close companions in Christian initiation.

LIVING AND DYING CHRISTIAN

Daily Public Prayer

The development of daily public prayer is vastly complicated. As we have seen, the New Testament makes reference to Christians praying constantly (Acts 1:14) but gives few details on corporate services. Our first references are to hours for prayer but they seem to be largely telling individual Christians when to pray. Clement of Alexandria, ca. 200, acknowledges that "some assign definite hours for prayer" yet argues that the true Christian "prays throughout his whole life." He also speaks of prayer in bodily terms: "we raise the head and lift the hands to heaven," a posture reflected in early Christian art. Tertullian prefers a regular discipline of prayer thrice during the day (on the basis of accounts of the apostles having prayed at the third, sixth, and ninth hours) plus prayer at daybreak and nightfall.

The *Apostolic Tradition* goes even further and recommends seven daily occasions for private prayer, the events of the crucifixion underlying the daytime hours. It also suggests the existence of a daily public gathering for instruction and prayer. This must have been difficult in times of persecution and the text suggests that it does not always take place.

The peace of the Church under Constantine changed all that and allowed daily services to flourish in many areas. A typical comment comes from Eusebius of Caesarea about 337 A.D.: "Rightly, it is no ordinary sign of the power of God, that throughout the whole world, in the churches of God, hymns, praises, and truly divine delights are offered to God at the morning going forth of the sun and at evening time."[15] The pattern this indicates appears in numerous churches. It is often called the cathedral office or people's office and reflects some important characteristics of popular religion. Highly repetitious, it consisted of favorite prayers, psalms, and hymns, all appropriate to the time of day. These began the day with hymns and prayers in the morning and psalms and prayers in the evening according to Epiphanius of Salamis (377). The *Apostolic Constitutions* prescribes the sixty-third psalm each morning and the hundred and forty-first each evening.

A daily cycle of morning and evening prayer for ordinary people developed, only to disappear in most parts of the world in later centuries. Chrysostom advises Christians "in the church at dawn to make your prayers and confessions" and for each one to return in the evening to "beg forgiveness for his falls." Egeria tells us of a series of daily prayer in Jerusalem with some hours for the monks and virgins and others for the clergy and lay people. These seem to include services at dawn, midday, three o'clock, and evening, with an extra service on Sunday before cockcrow. The services consist of prayers, psalms, and hymns. Light is brought in at the evening service or *lucernare*.

But another pattern of daily prayer was also evolving at the same time. This began with the development of monasticism in Egypt as a means of renouncing the world and even a Church grown worldly with respectability. Monasticism replaced martyrdom. Beginning in Egypt, men met daily to share in worship, consisting largely of psalms and prayers. Cassian tells us of that tradition by which an angelic visitant fixed at twelve the number of psalms at the night office and this became standard for much of the West.

In the mid-fourth century, Basil drew up a set of monastic rules for regulating the daily life of urban monastic groups. He noted eight daily occasions for prayer: early in the morning, at the third hour, at the sixth, at the ninth, when the day's work is ended, at nightfall, midnight, and before the dawn. The daytime hours, or little hours, or apostolic hours (from times noted in Acts) divide up the working day; the rest frame times of leisure and sleep. The old dilemma of how to pray without ceasing has been answered by devising a scheme for dividing the day into a series of services of praise and prayer. Obviously it could only be fulfilled by ascetics and people living in monastic community but Basil's rule has shaped the lives of thousands of eastern Christians in every generation from the fourth century until the present.

The western pattern was not firmly fixed until the sixth century. About 530, Benedict of Nursia produced his rule, based on older sources already in use. He, too, evolved a pattern of seven daily and one night offices: vespers at the end of the day, compline before bedtime, nocturns or vigils or matins early in the morning, lauds at daybreak, prime shortly thereafter, terce about nine, sext about noon, and none about three. He provided that "the whole psalter, of a hundred and fifty psalms, be sung every week, . . . our holy fathers bravely recited the Psalter in a single day; God grant that we, their degenerate sons, may do the like in seven."[16]

THE WESTERN MONASTIC CYCLE OF THE DAILY OFFICE

Vespers (at the end of the working day)
Compline (before bedtime)
Nocturns or **Vigils** or **Matins** (during middle of the night)
Lauds (at daybreak)
Prime (shortly thereafter)
Terce (during the middle of the morning)
Sext (at noon)
None (during middle of the afternoon)

DIAGRAM 2

As these words suggest, much of the choir office, daily office, *opus dei*, or liturgy of the hours consisted of the psalter. But added to that was a vast collection of prayers, hymns, readings from both testaments, readings from patristic sermons, legends of the saints, responses, and antiphons. It came to involve an assortment of books for the various readings, psalms, and musical items. As the essence of monastic life, it demanded full-time commitment although work was also esteemed as prayer. In all things, God was to be glorified whether at prayer or at work.

Ordinary people could not follow such a routine of prayer, and the history of the daily office in the west is a gradual disappearance of the people's office. Monasticism increasingly set the style for church architecture, church music, and the daily hours. What was happening as the popular religion of the people's office slipped out of sight was that daily prayer had become professionalized with the monks taking it over. Eventually local clergy followed monastic practices but left little prayer of a public nature for ordinary folk. The whole approach had become that of an athletic discipline, well suited to the needs of those intent on meditation and contemplation, but hardly suited for those raising a family. The disappearance of the people's office in the West was a tragedy for all. It left available only one model for daily public prayer: that of the monks.

The Eucharist

Our other tradition of daily and weekly public worship, the eucharist, has remained the central form of worship as far as the greatest number of Christians are concerned. It seems to have been a weekly event in the mid-second century in Rome. According to Justin Martyr, "on the day called Sunday there is a meeting in one place" for the eucharist. He then proceeds to give us our first outline of the entire service. It begins with the service of the word: "the memoirs of the apostles or the writings of the prophets are read as long as time permits."[17] Then follows the sermon and "we all stand up together and offer prayers." This is the first half of the eucharist, the service of the word as we know it today, consisting of readings from Old and New Testaments, a sermon, and prayer (presumably intercessory).

The second half, the service of the table, follows: bread and wine and water are brought (probably selected from that which members of the congregation have brought). Then the president "sends up prayers and thanksgivings to the best of his ability" or "as well as he is able," the congregation says "Amen," "and reception of the consecrated [elements] by each one takes place and they are sent to the absent by the deacons." Then an offering for the needy takes place. This tells us a number of things, chiefly that the eucharistic prayer is still spontaneous, not yet having received a fixed formula. There is still a high level of pastoral discretion, certainly in its wording, if not its contents as well. Some of the consecrated elements are set aside for those sick or in jail. The whole is seen in the context of providing for those in need. Justin also tells us only the baptized are allowed to partake and that "the food consecrated by the word of prayer . . . is the flesh and blood of that incarnate Jesus." He refers to the institution narratives from the "memoirs . . . called Gospels." Late in the same century, these words are reinforced by Irenaeus of Lyons: "The mixed cup and the bread that has been prepared receive the Word of God, and become the Eucharist, the body and blood of Christ."[18]

If Justin gives us the outline of the service (and some details and a little theology), it is left to the *Apostolic Tradition* in the next century to give us a much fuller account of the service of the table. It prescribes the actual text of the eucharistic prayer (canon, anaphora, or great thanksgiving) with words that have been borrowed by many of the western churches in recent years.

The *Apostolic Tradition* provides us accounts of two eucharists: one at the ordination of a bishop and the other at baptisms. The first includes a full text of the eucharistic prayer including the opening dialogue, thankful recital of the saving work of Christ including the institution narrative, a summary of what is recalled (*anámnesis*) and offering (oblation), an invocation (*epiclesis*) of the Holy Spirit on the offering and partakers, a concluding Trinitarian doxology, and an "Amen." Lacking is any suggestion of a *Sanctus* ("Holy, holy, holy") and a preface (preceding it and often reciting God's work of creation and the old covenant). But otherwise it is the pattern still widely in use in various churches today. It is addressed to the First member of the Trinity, recalls the work of the Second, and invokes the Third, all summed up in the doxology. Thanksgiving is made for God's previous works and there is supplication for God's action here and now. Modern prayers often sweep on from creation to the final consummation, encompassing all of history.

In the baptismal eucharist, *The Apostolic Tradition* gives us details of the distribution which on this occasion (only) includes three sips from three chalices: water (signifying inner baptism), milk and honey (signifying the promised land), and wine. The bread is given by the bishop with the words: "The bread of heaven in Christ Jesus." Also mentioned are the offering (presented by the deacons) and the breaking of the bread by the bishop. The service concludes quickly after receiving communion. The cup of milk and honey seems to have disappeared relatively soon. A different practice, the mixing of water with wine, has endured. Cyprian, a North African bishop, tells us in a letter of 253 A.D. that the mixing of water and wine signify the union of people with Christ since "the mixture cannot any more be separated."

For almost two hundred years, we know next to nothing about the development of the eucharist in Rome itself. But elsewhere in the fourth century, we see a wide array of advances both in texts and theological interpretations. One of the most prominent developments is the emergence of regional liturgies which are often classified in terms of families. Like human families, certain family characteristics similar to recognizable facial features persist in these. Usually the characteristics of the liturgy of a dominant regional city were absorbed by its neighbors but each passed on certain local features. These liturgical families are witnesses that the eucharist can have an essential unity but everywhere be expressed in the language and thought forms of a variety of peoples. Even the interpretations tend to reflect the various cultures in which they are articulated. The chief lesson we gain from these emerging liturgical families is how wide is the diversity of cultures which can comprehend unity in essentials but in their own terms. We shall look at the evidence of the eucharist from the fourth, fifth, and sixth centuries, going around the Mediterranean in a counter-clockwise direction.

Of the *North African family* we know very little other than a few matters about lectionaries since most of Christianity in this area was erased by Muslim conquests in the seventh century. Indications are, however, that there were strong links to Roman Christianity in worship as in other areas.

Our knowledge of Egyptian churches is more full, especially since Christians are still worshiping in Egyptian and Ethiopian churches. The association of the name of the evangelist St. Mark with Alexandria has given a name to this *St. Mark* or *Alexandrian family* although a fully developed liturgy for the patriarchate of Alexandria is not known until much later. Characteristic phrases include: "from sunrise to sunset, from north to south" and beginning the post-*sanctus* commemoration with the phrase "full in truth are heaven and earth of your holy glory," leading to a first epiclesis "fill, O God, this sacrifice." Even more distinctive is the long series of intercessions at the very beginning of the prayer, voicing the needs and aspirations of the people. "Bring the waters of the river [the Nile] to their proper measure; [by their rising] gladden [and renew] the face of the earth; water its furrows, multiply its fruits"[19] expresses a specifically Egyptian concern.

Further east, we encounter a family that centers around Jerusalem and Antioch, often called the *West Syrian* or *Antiochene family*. The archetypical liturgy is named for St. James, first bishop of Jerusalem, and probably reflects uses of both Antioch and Jerusalem. A particular fascination is apparent with the work of the Holy Spirit and it is invoked after the words of institution in fulsome language with a description of its activities that it "may come upon them . . . and make this bread the holy body of Christ . . . And this cup the precious blood of Christ." The same approach is reflected in Cyril's (or John's) mystagogical catecheses: "for whatsoever the Holy Ghost has touched, is sanctified and changed." This emphasis became a major liturgical and theological concern in Orthodox and oriental churches and was a major difference from the Roman Catholic and Protestant churches (until recently). The liturgy of St. James picks up after the *Sanctus* on the word "Holy." The prayer concludes with a long series of intercessions, each introduced by the phrase "Remember, Lord." Book 8 of the *Apostolic Constitutions*, probably from Syria about 375 A.D., contains our earliest full West Syran liturgy although it is unlikely it was ever used. If so, it would have required a very leisurely congregation for it relates a long narrative of the Old Testament before it even gets to the *Sanctus*. *Armenian* liturgies reflect patterns derived from the West Syrian family but with strong subsequent Byzantine influence.

Further east is a quite distinctive family, sometimes known as the *East Syrian family* or as the Liturgy of Saints Addai and Mari. It seems to have originated on the frontier between Rome and Persia in the city of Edessa sometime in the third century. Eventually, it reached as far as India and maybe China. It is the most Semitic in language, perhaps proof of its early date. Unlike other ancient rites, it appears to lack the words of institution although the priest may have recited them from memory.

Backtracking a bit, we run into the work of Basil (ca. 330–379), bishop of Caesarea in Asia Minor. He is credited with two eucharistic prayers. An early version, which he apparently took to Egypt, has been widely imitated in recent years by Protestants and Roman Catholics. A later version expanded on this and is still used in Orthodox churches on ten occasions a year. Both of Basil's eucharistic prayers follow a pattern similar to that of West Syria. The later version adds numerous scripture references and has a longer than usual post-*sanctus*, recounting the work of Christ in the new covenant.

Basil's liturgy forms part of the *Byzantine family* in addition to the Liturgy of *St. John Chrysostom*. It too, follows the West Syrian structure and reflects the same theology of consecration by the operation of the Holy Spirit. To the western ear, it sounds excessively verbose, poetic, and florid. Adjectives and attributes are piled up with relish: "For you are God, ineffable, inconceivable, invisible, incomprehensible, existing always and in the same way." The language has been likened to the oratorical flourishes of imperial court rhetoric or to neoplatonic mysticism. It breathes a different ethos from most western worship yet it apparently reveals a form of expression that has endeared itself to Greeks, Russians, and other eastern Christians.

Further west, we encounter the *Roman family* which was eventually to become the dominant family in the West. But in these early centuries there was little disposition to force areas beyond central Italy to conform with Roman use. We are looking in this period at a liturgical family fairly limited in geographic expanse although that was to change in the ninth century. Unfortunately, we do not know a great deal about its development in the third and fourth centuries.

Some things can be deduced from other sources. Ambrose gives us phrases in Milan which later appear in the Roman canon, indicating a common ancestor. Shifts in arrangement apparently happened during this period. The kiss of peace moved from the offertory to just before communion and Pope Gregory I is credited with fixing the Lord's Prayer at the end of the canon. Any epiclesis, such as in *Apostolic Tradition*, has disappeared. Various collections of mass texts, known as *libelli*, apparently were in circulation during the fourth to sixth centuries, providing fixed texts for various occasions. The spirit of the Roman rite has been compared to the down-to-business atmosphere of law courts; God is approached not as emperor but as judge. In a famous essay, Edmund Bishop asserts: "Mystery never flourished in the clear Roman atmosphere, and symbolism was no product of the Roman religious mind. . . . The genius of the Roman rite, . . . [is] soberness and sense."[20]

By contrast, the other *non-Roman Western families* were anything but concise and unimaginative. These are known collectively as Gallic families. Each has individual characteristics but we can make a few generalizations about the family tree. There seem to have been links to the churches of the east, ultimately deriving from the Antiochene pattern. The language tends to be poetic and imaginative; repetition abounds. "Soberness and sense" is not the native language of these people. Allusions and metaphors are rife; theological speculation abounds. Edmund Bishop compares a Roman preface for Pentecost, consisting of eight lines, with a Gallic one of eighty. Another common feature is a great variety of texts for different occasions with entire new eucharistic prayers for each unlike the Roman rite which changed only the preface of the eucharistic prayer.

We can only note a few details about each of these non-Roman Western families. We have already encountered Ambrose of Milan for whom the *Ambrosian or Milanese family* is named. Ambrose enunciates what was to become the standard western way of looking at consecration: "the priest no longer uses his own words, but he uses the words of Christ. Therefore the word of

Christ makes this Sacrament" just as his word created all things.[21] The emphasis is placed on the second person of the Trinity and on the words of institution; the Holy Spirit recedes from prominence.

The *Mozarabic family* originated in what is now Spain and Portugal. Unlike the Ambrosian family which today is used throughout the Archdiocese of Milan, the Mozarabic is confined to one chapel in the cathedral of Toledo, Spain. It, too, has a wide variety of texts, changing according to occasion.

The *Celtic family* comes from furthest afield, the monks of Ireland. Many of them became missionaries to the continent and brought this use to the Rhineland and points as distant as northern Italy. It has not been in use for many centuries.

Probably the widest use was that of the *Gallican family* in much of what now is France and Germany. It has the same relish for variety, imagination, speculation, and florid language. Though it no longer survives by itself, many of its prayers were eventually incorporated into the Roman rite and survive today there and in several Protestant traditions, such as the Episcopal and Methodist "Collect for Purity" at the beginning of the eucharist. Thus, though most of these non-Roman western rites have been laid aside, some parts are still in use.

Christian Time

Our account of the keeping of time is directly connected with the eucharist. As we have seen, Justin Martyr associates the eucharist with Sunday. His reasons are explicit: "We all hold this common gathering on Sunday, since it is the first day, on which God transforming darkness and matter made the universe, and Jesus Christ our Saviour rose from the dead on the same day."[22] The pagan term, day of the sun, is adopted unashamedly. The *Epistle of Barnabas* (late first or second century) calls Sunday the eighth day, or start of a new creation in Christ. By the mid-second century, the eucharist and Sunday are firmly and permanently linked. Both commemorate creation (which begins with the creation of light (Gen. 1:3-5) and resurrection.

The structure of the Christian week is outlined two centuries before the contours of the Christian year become apparent. (We have already discussed the shape of the Christian day in terms of daily public prayer.) Sunday, of course, was the chief liturgical day. Not until Constantine did it also become a day of rest. For city dwellers (but not farmers), it became legally a day of rest in 321.

The *Didache* had mandated fasting on Wednesdays and Fridays but by the late fourth century better reasons had been found than outdoing the hypocrites. The *Apostolic Constitutions* (ca. 375) commands fasting on Wednesdays because of Judas' betrayal and on Friday because of the crucifixion. Tertullian tells us that Christians do not kneel in prayer on Sunday. There are still a few around who do not kneel on the Sabbath either but such observances disappear soon thereafter. Thus the week is well defined and has kept its shape ever since.

The evolution of the Christian year was a slower, much more complicated process, many details of which are still mysterious. Christianity inherited from Judaism two great festivals: Passover (Pascha) and Pentecost. These were retained in Christianity but with new meanings: the Messiah had come at the Passover in a way hardly expected and the law (which the Jewish Pentecost commemorated) had been replaced by the advent of the Spirit.

The third great festival, Epiphany, is the most puzzling as to origins.[23] It is clearly not Jewish. One theory is that it originated in Egypt where it apparently was observed by a group of Egyptian gnostics, the Basilidians, as early as the mid-second century but is mentioned shortly thereafter by orthodox Christians. There is much debate about whether Epiphany originally commemorated the birth of Jesus (with which Matthew and Luke begin) or the baptism of the Lord (the start of Mark and John). It also developed connections with the first of Jesus' miracle signs, that at the wedding feast at Cana (John 2:11). Other theories place the dating (January 6) as nine months after his death and conception (both once thought to be on April 6). And it is possible that January 6 marks the date of the beginning of the yearly cycle of gospel readings at worship.

The history of these three great festivals—Epiphany, Passover, and Pentecost—shows some common factors. Originating as unitive festivals, they are splintered into several commemorations in the course of the fourth century. And the ensuing results have remained much the same ever since.

The Pascha originally commemorated all the events of Holy Week and Easter Week in a single day which became the chief occasion for baptism, since it reflects death and resurrection. It seems almost certain that the dissolution of this unitive celebration occurred in Jerusalem in the fourth century where many pilgrims came to worship. Having the sites of the events narrated in scripture, it is only natural that services were created to reenact the central events of the paschal mystery. Egeria, who visited there about 384, tells us in considerable detail how on Palm Sunday "the bishop and all the people . . . start off on foot down from the summit of the Mount of Olives . . . with psalms and antiphons, . . . repeating, 'Blessed is he that cometh in the name of the Lord.'"[24] The gospels provide the script for the rest of the week. On Wednesday, the betrayal is commemorated; Thursday sees a visit to Gethsemane; and on Friday people file by to kiss the wood of the true cross. Not long thereafter, Augustine in North Africa could state with certainty "it is clear from the Gospel on what days the Lord was crucified and rested in the tomb and rose again."[25] Ever since the fourth century, Christians have kept the sacred triduum (three days) beginning at nightfall on Thursday as Good Friday, Holy Saturday (or Easter Eve), and Easter Day. To these were added Palm (now Passion/Palm) Sunday, Spy Wednesday, and Maundy (or Holy) Thursday. What made perfect sense in Jerusalem because of the conjunction of places and times was soon observed wherever Christians went.

A controversy endured well into the fifth century among a group of Asian conservatives, known as Quartodecimans. As early as the second century, they insisted on observing Easter according to the Jewish dating of the Passover, i.e., on the fourteenth of the month of Nisan which might come on any day of the week. They may represent the earliest Christian practice, but eventually all Christians came to celebrate Easter only on Sunday.

The division of Pentecost and Ascension Day is less easy to pinpoint as to locale. Eusebius, writing about 338 A.D. speaks of "that one day on which the holy Scriptures attest the ascension of our common Saviour into heaven, and the descent of the Holy

Spirit among men."[26] But within fifty years or so the *Apostolic Constitutions* matter of factly tells us that one counts forty days (Acts 1:3) after Easter to the day of the ascension and session at God's right hand. And so we still observe it.

The division of the birth festivals is puzzling. Suddenly, in addition to Epiphany, we hear of a new festival, the birth of Christ in Bethlehem of Judea, probably originating in Rome about 336 A.D., although there may be earlier evidence from North Africa. Fifty years later, Chrysostom in Antioch found it necessary to explain Christmas as a new and unfamiliar festival to his flock. But eventually Christmas prevailed and Epiphany came to reflect, for the West, the visit of the Magi. Once the date of the birth was fixed at December 25, it was relatively easy on the basis of scripture and biology to date the Annunciation nine months earlier (March 25), Circumcision on January 1 eight days after birth (Luke 2:21), and Presentation in the Temple (or Purification or Candlemas) on February 2 after forty days (Luke 2:22-40). Mary's Visitation of Elizabeth was placed at May 31 (Luke 1:39-56), shortly before the birth of John the Baptist (June 24).

All these festivals formed both the calendar of the fourth century and of the twentieth as well. As early as the second century, local churches began to observe the anniversary of the death (or heavenly birthday) of local heroes and heroines of the faith, what we would call today saints' days. These involved readings of the saint's life and proper prayers.

The three main festivals soon developed extensions over a period of time, a single day not seeming sufficient. Tertullian tells us of the great fifty days during which "the resurrection of the Lord was repeatedly proved among the disciples" as a time of great joy. We call it the Easter Season; the early Church called it Pentecost (fifty days) and read the book of Acts during it as the "proof of the resurrection."

Lent is a bit more puzzling. Functionally it serves as a preparation period for those about to be baptized at Easter, as the *Apostolic Tradition* suggests. But it may have originated as a forty day fast after the baptism of the Lord on Epiphany just as Jesus went into the wilderness after his baptism (Luke 4:2) and fought temptation. In time, Lent came to apply to all Christians as a time of preparation for Easter. The Council of Nicaea speaks of it in 325 as the "forty" [days], and Cyril tells those chosen for baptism in Jerusalem "you have a long period of grace, forty days for repentance." Augustine sees Lent as a reflection of the fasts of Moses and Elijah as well as the Lord.

A similar development occurred with regard to the birth festivals. An early stage is represented by a three-week period before Epiphany, perhaps eventually extended backwards to make forty days, and then terminated by the new feast, Christmas. The result is a four-week Season of Advent.

So what we have is a year of two cycles, nativity and paschal, consisting of four seasons: Advent and Christmas, Lent and Easter plus the intervals in between. It is not particularly neat and tidy but it has rung true to the Christian experience of the gospel and functioned very well ever since the fourth century. Only a handful of lesser commemorations were added in subsequent centuries and we can regard development of the Christian year as virtually complete by the fifth century.

Pastoral Rites

That can hardly be said of the various pastoral rites, several of which are still changing.

1. Reconciliation. During this period, the problem of what to do with flagrant sinners began to be resolved in a systematic fashion. Penance came to be required of those committing major sins by insisting on a public once-in-a-lifetime occurrence process. This was only for those few who did a good job of being bad, not for ordinary sinners. One of our earliest treatises on what became a sacrament is a long essay Tertullian wrote in about 203 *On Penance.* He calls it a plank after shipwreck but notes that those who endure shipwreck and live henceforth "declare divorce with ship and sea." Penance or *exomologésis* is a public period of prostration and humiliation, wearing mean clothes, tasting little food, and much weeping. But it is far better to be purged in public before humans than damned in secret before God. Penance is medicinal and like bitter medicine it is effective for the soul.

The public nature of this type of penance is partly dictated by the fact that one has offended the community as well as God and indeed in times of persecution made it more vulnerable. So one is reconciled to the community and to God. This came to be signified at the end of Lent when penitents were reunited to the community that had expelled them from its eucharist just as the newly baptized were being united to the church.

Because of the severe nature of public penance, it was allowed only once in a lifetime and many sinners were not reconciled and given communion until they were at death's door. Major changes were to occur in the whole process in the next period.

2. *Healing*. The healing of the sick continued for several centuries to be associated with anointing with oil and healing by lay people. Oil blessed by a bishop was used but it was rubbed on the skin wherever the pain was or taken internally by the sufferer or applied to that person by a friend. We have a fourth-century prayer from Sarapion, bishop of Thmuis in Egypt that reads: we "pray thee to send healing power of the only-begotten from heaven upon this oil, that it may become to those who are being anointed (with it) or partaking of these thy creatures, for a throwing off of every sickness and every infirmity, for a charm against every demon."[27] The purpose is clearly healing and any Christian can minister the blessed oil and pray for others who are afflicted. It is a ministry of great love open to all Christians and clearly presumes the possibility of healing. All that was to change in time.

3. *Christian Marriage*. Rites largely tended to reflect local customs. The churches were concerned that Christians marry other Christians and that had been (and is) a problem from Paul on. Many pagan Roman customs simply were adopted and are with us even today. They simply were purged of those items contaminated by idolatry, e.g., fire the soothsayer but keep the veil, the ring, the joining of hands, the public consent, and the wedding feast. Since marriage is common to all peoples, it is not strange that the provisions of local cultures were treated so sympathetically.

Only slowly was the process Christianized, chiefly by blessing of the bride at the veiling or joining of hands, or at the bridal chamber. The blessings tended to dwell on the example of holy married women of the Old Testament (skipping over the bigamous couples) and dwelling on the Christ-Church model of

Ephesians 5. But marriages were still primarily private ceremonies and it took another thousand years to get the whole occasion inside the church building.

4. Christian Burial. The burial of Christians again reflected local customs but with some important differences. Roman pagan funerals tended to be at night with black clothing, professional mourners, and flute players, and ended in cremation. By contrast, the Christian funeral was in daylight, white was worn, and the procession sang psalms, especially 22, 23, and 116, on the way to the cemetery where burial took place. The procession dominates the rite and the imagery is that of a Roman triumph, a victorious hero welcomed home.

Yet many Roman practices endured. The *refrigerium* was a meal on the burial site which united the family and the deceased. A eucharist might be celebrated at the graveside as Augustine tells us was done at the burial of his mother, Monica, in 387. The inviolability of graves, even of those executed by the state, long endured. The invasion of barbarians in the fifth century and the threat to tombs outside the city walls led to the removal, for safe keeping, of the relics of saints. The dominant image of Christian funerals, unlike those of other people, was the sense of hope for those who had died in the Lord. The focus was not on human sin but on God's victory in Jesus Christ.

LIVING TOGETHER IN COMMUNITY

Church life became infinitely more complex in this period, especially after Constantine. The authority of major ecclesiastical centers such as Alexandria, Constantinople, and Rome increased considerably. We shall examine four areas of communal development in worship: leadership, preaching, music, and architecture.

Leadership

Leadership became more systematic and rigidly structured, and moved increasingly in a hierarchical direction. The chief exception was the earliest Irish church where monasticism prevailed and abbots were the chief authority figures, even over the large numbers of wandering bishops. Most monks at this time were laymen. The prophets who figure so prominently in first-century documents disappear rather quickly in favor of a ministry of those in orders. The chief exception is the prophets and prophetesses of the second and third-century Montanist sect.

There is still some latitude in the *Apostolic Tradition* since confessors who have been imprisoned for the Lord need no further act to become presbyters. Ordination is not implied for widows, readers, virgins, subdeacons, and healers because "ordination is for the clergy, on account of their liturgical duties." But ordination has become well regulated, at least in third century Rome.

In the *Apostolic Tradition* the bishop is ordained by other bishops but "chosen by all the people . . . named and accepted by all." After everyone has given assent, one bishop lays hands on the person being ordained. The ordination prayer recites God's calls to ministry from the time of Abraham to the apostles then turns to asking the Father to send the Spirit to empower the new bishop to fulfill the job description which forms the second half of the prayer. The new bishop then presides at the eucharist. In the case of a presbyter, the bishop lays hands on his head together with the other presbyters, invoking the Father to send the Holy Spirit to make him "worthy to minister." But for deacons, only the bishop lays on hands, invoking the Holy Spirit. It is clear that the deacons' functions are service of the bishop. These ordination prayers have been widely imitated in recent revisions.

The *Apostolic Tradition* and other church orders mention several additional offices, ordained and not. The most intriguing question is over the ordination of deaconesses. As we have seen, the *Didascalia Apostolorum* notes the need for them at baptism. In the following century, the *Apostolic Constitutions* includes a rite for laying on of hands on a deaconess with a prayer, listing God's work in Miriam, Deborah, Anna, and Huldah, mentioning that God "also in the tent of the testimony and in the temple appointed women to be guardians of your holy gates,"[28] then invokes the Holy Spirit on her. The Byzantine rite of a somewhat later date reminds God: "not to men alone but also to women [you] bestowed grace and the advent of your Holy Spirit" and then proceeds to ask "send down upon her the abundant gift of your Holy Spirit."[29] In the fourth-century *Testamentum Domini*, widows are ordained.[30]

Sarapion, in fourth-century Egypt, has prayers for the three orders and credits God with creating orders of bishops, presbyters, and deacons. He likens deacons to the seven (Acts 6:3-6), calls presbyters stewards and ambassadors, and sees the bishop as successor of the holy apostles and a shepherd to God's flock. In other early texts, a variety of what later were called minor orders appears, especially readers and subdeacons. In the *Testamentum Domini*, subdeacons are ordained, but readers are not; in the *Canons of Hippolytus* of the same century subdeacons and healers both are ordained but in the *Apostolic Tradition* none of these receive orders. The three orders of deacons, priests, and bishops are consistently ordained in all these documents.

Preaching

Preaching had always been a part of Christianity but in this period it became a highly skilled art form and a vital part of worship. Numerous sermons survive to testify to this great age of pulpit rhetoric. Even the pulpit itself is said to have originated in the decision of John Chrysostom to preach from the reading desk instead of remaining seated in the presider's chair. The pulpit developed into an important liturgical center and has remained that ever since.

The preachers of the patristic period borrowed from pagan culture the rhetorical skills developed over centuries. Augustine had been a student of rhetoric in Carthage and then teacher of it in Rome. Christians were familiar with a great tradition of persuasive public speaking. It had become no mean science and the forms and methods of public address contributed directly to the evolution of the Christian sermon.

At the same time, biblical exegesis was developing to give content to what preachers had to say. In the third century, Origen and others wrote biblical commentaries and various schools of interpretation developed, especially in Alexandria and Antioch. Though preaching may not have been their only purpose, these commentators helped develop ways of dealing with even the most obscure of biblical texts. Lectionaries were in use by the fourth century to dictate the lessons read and texts preached on throughout the year. The reading of Acts during the Easter Season is attested to in various regions. By the time of Pope Gregory I, a standard series of pericopes had stabilized in Rome for the Sundays and feast days of the year and has remained in use until recently.

The fourth and fifth centuries produced some of the greatest preachers of all time: Augustine, Ambrose, Jerome, Cyril, Chrysostom, Leo I, to name a few. In some cases, scribes took down the words, and many sermons from this period still read well. One soon realizes why John Chrysostom was named "golden-mouthed." But he was not alone and this was one of the great eras of the preached word in worship. Even pagans came to hear the service of the word and Augustine himself was converted largely through the eloquence of Ambrose's preaching.

Church Music

Although we have plenty of sermons, we have no notations for music from this period but plenty of evidence for its use in worship. There were always problems associated with music as long as paganism survived since Christians wanted to dissociate themselves from pagan singing and musical instruments. Not only was pagan music enticing; even Jewish music was problematic, especially since Christians delighted in singing the psalms which frequently made mention of an assortment of musical instruments, some of which Christians prohibited.

Early Christian worship music was sung in unison. Many early writers consider this singing "with one voice" as itself a testimony to the unity of members within the body. The words could be both psalms and hymns, often sung responsorally. Egeria tells us frequently of psalms and hymns in the worship in Jerusalem and remarks: "At each of these occasions the psalms and antiphons they have are appropriate to the place and the day."[31] Her whole narrative is filled with mention of hymns, antiphons, and psalms. The monks and virgins and also some lay people fill the time between cockcrow and daybreak every day "in singing the refrains to the hymns, psalms, and antiphons." It is certainly musical liturgy.

There are abundant references to women singers, choirs of virgins, and quite likely, female cantors. But this was not without difficulties, partly because of association with women singers at pagan feasts and partly because women singers were prominent in some heretical groups. So in different areas, depending upon the ruling anxieties, women singers were forbidden. Boy choirs also had a role and are mentioned in the *Testamentum Domini* which speaks of "the virgins alternating with the boys responding to the one who sings the psalms in the church." Obviously, singing had become a highly organized matter by this time.

But music could be controversial, too. Augustine confesses how greatly he enjoyed the singing in the church of Milan and how much this contributed to his conversion but at the same time has fears that singing is too attractive. He ponders having music banished: "I vacillate between dangerous pleasure and healthful exercise. I am inclined—though I pronounce no irrevocable opinion on the subject—to approve of the use of singing in church, so that by the delights of the ear the weaker minds may be stimulated to a devotional mood."[32] Some branches of eastern monasticism went much further in a negative fashion, denying that singing and piety were compatible. But in general, singing was an important part of worship in this period.

Various writers composed the many hymns, most famous of which are those of Ambrose. His "O Splendor of God's Glory Bright" is still sung today as are those of sixth-century Venantius Fortunatus: "Sing, My Tongue, the Glorious Battle" and "Hail Thee, Festival Day." In theological controversies, such as with the Arians, hymns were a favorite form of theological propaganda for both sides. The power of hymn singing as a teaching tool as well as praise of God was certainly recognized. And hymn singing had the advantage of a high degree of congregational participation.

Church Architecture

The most striking change of all in this period came in the area of architecture. After the peace of the church made building legal,

Christian worship went from a furtive secret affair to a spectacular public event and a different architectural setting was needed.

There were churches built, to be sure, before Constantine. His predecessor, Diocletian, had had one destroyed in Nicomedia because it overshadowed imperial buildings. And court cases and records of floods reveal the existence of others built when persecution was relaxed. But in general, it was safer for Christians to worship in private homes during much of the first three centuries. The earliest surviving house church dates from 232–256 in Dura-Europos, a frontier garrison town on the Euphrates. In it, an ordinary house has been adapted by throwing together two rooms and raising a small platform at one end, presumably for the altar-table. Another room has a baptistry built so children could be immersed or adults washed by pouring. The baptistry room is decorated with biblical murals such as the women at the empty tomb. Thus early we see distinct liturgical spaces being allocated for different acts of worship and appropriate liturgical centers provided for each. Other rooms were probably used for catechesis. Dura-Europos must have been typical of thousands of other clandestine house churches.

Under Constantine, two models of public buildings were available: the pagan temple and the civil basilica. The temple was useless for it was designed so only the priests entered it, the people and sacrifices being on the exterior. The civil basilica, usually a longitudinal building with a row of columns on each side of the interior supporting clerestory windows, terminated in a semi-circular apse. It could easily be adapted for Christian worship. The bishop simply took the place of the judge on the throne in the apse, flanked by presbyters. In front of him stood the altar-table, free standing, and rather small by later standards. Wooden ones gave way to stone. Eventually, low screens railed in a space in front of it for the singers, and an ambo (pulpit) accommodated readings. The rest was open congregational space where the people stood, usually divided by sexes. For well over a thousand years, the posture of worship was standing. The bishop presided facing the people over the altar-table and preached from his throne until the locus shifted to the pulpit.

Baptistries were frequently built as separate buildings nearby, often on the model of a mausoleum with the pool at the center. Shrines for the relics of saints took a similar form when relics began to be moved about from place to place from the fifth century on.

In such a strange new setting, there was a rapid growth in ceremonial, with many aspects of the imperial court being adopted; incense, processional lights, and ceremonial fans became common. The change in scale from tiny homes to vast basilicas was enormous. Constantine himself donated or built basilicas in Rome, Constantinople, Jerusalem, and Bethlehem. A whole new vocabulary of gesture, vesture, and visual art had to be learned.

Most of our earliest surviving liturgical art was associated with burial of the dead. Not surprisingly, it featured resurrection themes, often in Old Testament terms: Jonah and the whale, Daniel and the boys in the fiery furnace, the raising of Lazarus. Occasionally Christ is portrayed as the Good Shepherd or the Church as a praying woman. The cross does not appear until the fourth century and then often with a lamb on it. Not until the end of the seventh century do we discover the familiar crucifix. After the Marian debates at the Council of Ephesus in 431, figures of Mary became prominent. The churches were learning a new visual vocabulary, one image at a time. By the end of the patristic period many images had become familiar for visual expression in worship.

The end of this period marks mammoth development in every aspect of Christian worship since the time of the New Testament. Much of the legacy of this time is still with us today. Many of the reforms in worship in the last twenty-five years draw deeply from the wells of this period.

FOR FURTHER READING

Davies, J. G. *The Origin and Development of Early Christian Architecture.* New York: Philosophical Library, 1953.

Dix, Gregory. *The Shape of the Liturgy*. Westminster: Dacre Press, 1945.

Foley, Edward. *From Age to Age: How Christians Celebrated the Eucharist*. Chicago: Liturgy Training Publications, 1991.

Guiver, George. *Company of Voices: Daily Prayer and the People of God*. New York: Pueblo Publishing Company, 1988.

Jones, Cheslyn, Geoffrey Wainwright, Edward Yarnold, and Paul Bradshaw, editors. *The Study of Liturgy*. Revised edition. New York: Oxford University Press, 1992.

Jungmann, Josef. *The Early Liturgy to the Time of Gregory the Great*. Notre Dame: University of Notre Dame Press, 1959.

———. *Pastoral Liturgy*. New York: Herder and Herder, 1962.

Klauser, Theodor. *A Short History of the Western Liturgy*. Second edition. Oxford: Oxford University Press, 1979.

Martimort, A. G., editor. *The Church at Prayer*. New edition. Collegeville: Liturgical Press, 1986–1988. 4 volumes.

Rordorf, Willy. *Sunday: The History of the Day of Rest and Worship*, Philadelphia: Westminster Press, 1968.

Rowell, Geoffrey. *The Liturgy of Christian Burial*. London: Alcuin Club/S.P.C.K., 1977.

Stevenson, Kenneth. *Nuptial Blessing*. London: Alcuin Club/S.P.C.K., 1982.

Talley, Thomas J. *The Origins of the Liturgical Year*. Second, Emended edition. Collegeville: Liturgical Press, 1991.

Wegman, Hermann. *Christian Worship in East and West*. New York: Pueblo Publishing Company, 1985.

Worship in the Churches of the Middle Ages

We turn now to look at the history of Christian worship as it developed over the Middle Ages. This is a vast period of time, roughly 600 to 1500. For convenience, it is sometimes divided into two segments: the Early Middle Ages from 604 (death of Gregory I) to 1085 (death of Gregory VII) and the Late Middle Ages from 1085 to 1517 (Luther's 95 theses). Even this is of little help since change was continuous, more rapid in some places than others, but nevertheless constant. Each century has its own distinctive flavor. The best we can hope to do is to trace a few major trajectories. But this has certain advantages since most developments, once started, are consistent; reversals are uncommon.

We are also dealing with an ever-expanding geography. North Africa and much of Spain were lost to Muslims, to be sure, but Christianity expanded to the North and East when the South was blocked. Missionaries reached Iceland ca. 980 and eventually a cathedral and parish churches were found even amid Greenland's icy mountains. Northern Europe and Scandinavia were converted, Norway by the mid-eleventh century, Sweden and Finland by the mid-twelfth. Progress to the east for the Orthodox churches was equally spectacular, the conversion of Ukraine and Russia beginning in earnest in 988. At the same time, the Great Schism of 1054 permanently divided East and West and insult was added to injury when western crusaders sacked Constantinople in 1204. Even worse was to befall the East in 1453 when the patriarchal city of Constantinople fell to Muslims as long before had Alexandria, Jerusalem, and Antioch. This gave the West further incentives to look westward, a dream fulfilled in unexpected ways in 1492 by contact with American civilizations.

This is a period of enormous importance for the study of Protestant worship. Protestants share the heritage of this period in common with Roman Catholics. Both inherited western forms of Christian worship and the resulting developments are often more similar to one another than to eastern forms. On some items, Protestants might be more conservative, retaining items that baroque Catholicism tended to jettison. We shall argue that a penitential eucharistic piety was one of these. Luther and his heirs never got past the medieval idea of a wide variety of local usages even when Catholicism looked to liturgical standardization. And various Protestant reformers brought to their logical conclusion some medieval developments such as the final splintering of initiation or reliance on the words of institution to consecrate the eucharist. In many ways, the sixteenth-century reformers have more in common with the churches of the Middle Ages than with the churches of modern times. Many medieval pieties and practices remained intact in Protestantism because they were the only models available when reforming items such as daily public prayer. The medieval roots are essential to understanding Protestant worship.

THE WORLD OF THE MIDDLE AGES

The nineteenth century tended to see the Middle Ages, as G. K. Chesterton said, "by moonlight." When we subject the period to the bright noonday light of modern scholarship the results appear far less engaging. Medieval life, to use Hobbes' famous phrase, was "nasty, and brutish, and short" although not without redeeming features. But with poor nutrition, the average life span had shrunk to less than half the biblical three score and ten and even the average body size had shrunk considerably since classical times. Most people lived in villages of modest size. Even the biggest cities were tiny by modern size and nothing came close to the million inhabitants of imperial Rome. For most people, liturgical life centered in their parish church, served by a priest or two and several men in minor orders. Dioceses were vast north of Italy and the majority of people never got near a bishop. The logistics of visiting as many as eight hundred parishes in a diocese, the primitive condition of roads, and the civil occupations of bishops made encounters with the average parishioner unlikely.

Life was frequently cut short because of civil turmoil. The whole period is rife with strife whether it was invasion of Norsemen or warring neighbors. Slowly order emerged out of chaos but this often only increased the scale of conflict. Much of Europe was organized to fight crusades in the twelfth and thirteenth centuries and Christians held Jerusalem for just over a hundred years. But the next step was to imperial and national wars. Plagues also cut life short. The black death of 1353 decimated the population; many villages never recovered.

In the midst of such fragile life there was one center of social stability, monastic life. Western monasticism, exclusively Benedictine until such reform movements as the Cluniac in the tenth century and the Cistercian in the twelfth, provided a safe haven for many of the intellectual and spiritual currents of each century. Even the monks were not totally immune from war and disease but they achieved such security as was possible. Through difficult times, they kept the lamp of learning lighted and many monasteries had a scriptorum where manuscript books were laboriously produced. Above all else, monks were people whose prime occupation was worship. The daily and night office eventually took a major part of their time and became a worship style admirably fitted to their contemplative and meditative life.

For better or worse, the monks set the agenda for much of medieval worship and we can speak of a monastic hegemony of worship. Their impact on the daily office was obvious but they did much to shape the growth of church music at which they were the masters. Church architecture came very much under their sway. The monks built the largest medieval church (Cluny) and buildings designed for monastic worship were imitated everywhere from cathedrals to the smallest parish church. The advent of the new mendicant orders (Franciscans, Dominicans, Carmelites, Servites) in the thirteenth century brought about further liturgical influences especially in preaching and in liturgical books. Most liturgical changes in the Middle Ages seem to originate from the religious orders.

Out of these communities and cathedral schools developed the medieval university and its houses of study, many sponsored by religious orders. With beginnings in the late twelfth century, by the thirteenth universities led the revival of learning as monastics had once done. The thirteenth century saw major contributions of scholastic theologians in helping the churches to make up their minds about what Christians experienced in worship. This produced very sophisticated definitions of the sacraments, perhaps too sophisticated because they treated the sacraments, now narrowed to seven in number, in terms of intellectual categories rather than as awesome mysteries. The down side of doctrinal development was the institution of the inquisition to deal with Christians whose beliefs passed beyond accepted boundaries and with Jews. The treatment of the latter led to their expulsion from some countries (England in 1290, Spain in 1492) and presaged the holocaust of our century.

In the midst of all these changes, the liturgical role of Rome was far from deliberate. Because of the prestige accorded the holy city as the resting place of the martyrs, Roman ways of worship were widely imitated even though Rome rarely sought to promote them outside of nearby regions of Italy. Essentially the Roman liturgical spirit was a conservative one. As we have seen in an earlier period with Egeria in Jerusalem, pilgrims are inclined to be very observant. What they notice they tend to replicate when they get back home. Pilgrims to Rome throughout the Middle Ages were no less observant. Of course they came to Rome to see the pope and the principal stational churches, not presbyters in ordinary parish churches. And so what they tended to take home were chiefly memories of papal ceremonial.

Romanitas or the imitation of Rome as the most impressive model for liturgy became a common western practice. Many practices originating north of the Alps were imposed on Rome itself during the nadir of its influence in the tenth century. Monastic orders, especially after the centralization that Cluny and Citeaux represented, became effective means of propagating these additions to Roman practices. This process repeated itself with the roving mendicant orders of the thirteenth century.

But for the most part, Rome took a hands off approach. Its influence was largely from respect not from coercion. Charlemagne tried to use liturgy as a means of unifying his empire in the ninth century but with little cooperation from Rome. Gregory VII interfered in the worship of the Spanish churches in the eleventh century by trying to force relinquishment of the Mozarabic rite in favor of the Roman rite but with only partial success. Most of his successors were less adamant and closer to Gregory I in allowing local rites to thrive. Liturgical centralization was impossible in any case before the invention of the printing press. As late as 1549, Cranmer noted England still had various uses: "some following Salisbury use, some Hereford use, some of the use of Bangor, some of York, and some of Lincoln."

BECOMING CHRISTIAN

Initiation followed two quite different trajectories in East and West as we have already seen. In the East, initiation was held together at all costs as a single occasion. Our oldest text for the Byzantine rite is the *Barberini Euchologion* from about 790. But it is redolent of the language of John Chrysostom himself, linking it to the late fourth century. It contains prayers for naming infants on the eighth day after birth. Then on the fortieth day they are ritually made a catechumen and exorcised, water is blessed as is oil, the candidates are anointed with the oil of gladness, baptized, and they receive anointing with the sign of the cross and the words "the seal of the gift of the Holy Spirit." Then the eucharist begins and the newly baptized receive communion.

As new areas in the East were Christianized, baptism of infants became the normal practice after the first generation. The whole process varied little whatever the age. Infants, of course, could only receive the wine in the eucharist but it was possible to wash them from head to foot. The entire rite could be carried out by a priest using oil blessed by a bishop for the final anointing which came to be called chrismation. These practices have been followed with little change right down to the present. A temporary challenge came from a dualistic sect known as Bogomiles who may have been the first group to cease the practice of infant baptism. They flourished in the Balkans and Asia Minor in the twelfth century but eventually disappeared. But they hardly affected the resolute course of Orthodoxy to retain the integrity of initiation regardless of age.

The pattern of the West was far less consistent. It is a story of slow but irreversible division of the process of initiation into three occasions, often separated by years, and usually involving two or three different orders of ministers. In this development, theology was hard pressed to interpret what was actually happening in practice.

One of our earliest records is the *Gelasian Sacramentary*, parts of which may date from the late fifth century. Here the rite still possesses its integral character and furthermore is associated with Easter or Pentecost. There is a series of three scrutinies performed during Lent in which the candidates are prepared for baptism even though it is apparent that many are infants. On the day of their baptism occurs the *effeta*, renunciation, exorcism, blessing of the water, baptism, anointing, laying on of hands by the bishop, and mass with communion.

Contrast that with the statement at the end of the Middle Ages in the 1566 *Catechism of Trent*: "Until children shall have attained the age of reason, its [confirmation] administration is inexpedient. If not, therefore to be postponed to the age of twelve, it is most proper to defer this Sacrament at least to that of seven years."[1] All Protestant groups that retained confirmation inherited the same expectations.

Nevertheless, the dissolution was a long protracted process. As late as 1533, we note that Princess Elizabeth I was baptized and confirmed three days after birth. Several quite different factors were at work to break apart the original unity.

Although the eastern churches still give communion to newly baptized babies, this came to be a problem for the West. As we shall shortly see, by the twelfth century there was a growing scrupulosity in the West over the communion elements and fear that any crumb or drop might be profaned by being dropped or spilled. As late as the eleventh century, Lanfranc, Archbishop of Canterbury, staunchly defended infant communion. The usual practice was that of dipping the priest's finger in the chalice and then placing it on the infant's lips. The twelfth century developed the doctrine of concomitance to show that the entire Christ was received whether from bread or wine, no matter how large the portion. Fear of spilling the blessed blood led to an unwillingness to receive the wine by laity of any age, not just at baptism. By the time of the Fourth Lateran Council (1215), confession was made mandatory before communion, mute witness that communion at baptism had not only disappeared but apparently had been altogether forgotten. But it is important for contemporary debates that for nearly twelve centuries, both West and East were agreed that communion was a part of initiation. Infant communion has a long, if forgotten, history throughout Christendom.

One of the most obvious aspects of initiation, at least by the fourth century, was its strong paschal nature. Initiation was tied to Easter or Pentecost, either end of the great fifty days of Easter. The presumption was that it be administered at those times and by the bishop. But theology was to intervene. Augustine's teaching on the necessity of baptism to cancel the guilt of original sin won the day. For who would risk a child's salvation by postponing baptism? If the child died a day after baptism, its salvation was assured; if it died a day before, it could in no wise enter the kingdom of heaven (John 3:5). The consequences were clear; no one would wait a few months until Easter for baptism if that might endanger the infant's eternal salvation. From the fourteenth century onward, councils and synods decreed baptism should occur within eight days of birth. Not only did this rush effectively abolish any connection with the paschal season but eliminated the likelihood that a bishop would be available to administer it. The rite might still suggest that baptism was for adults and even included relics of the enrollment of catechumens but infant baptism soon after birth became the norm.

By contrast, the interval between baptism and confirmation increased greatly. Practical problems of access to a bishop made confirmation unlikely for most people at whatever age. There are stories of bishops passing through villages while confirming from horseback. Although confirmation was highly desirable, as long as the West limited it to being done by bishops, it could never be considered necessary to salvation as was baptism. The theologians wrestled over what practice had engendered. It was hard to tell what confirmation gave that baptism had not already conveyed but the scholastic arguments were that confirmation augmented the grace of baptism or that it provided strength to fight evil. Gradually it came to be acknowledged that confirmation must wait until the age of reason, usually set at seven. And with this division, the unity of initiation for the West was lost, if not forever, at least until recent times.

Can we then make any generalizations at all about initiation in this long period of time? A few seem reasonably safe. Except for those who lived in cathedral cities, baptism was in the parish church. There was a tradition of the baptistry as a separate building in Italy and a few examples remain in other countries. But the prevailing medieval setting was a baptismal font immediately inside the main entrance to the church. This allowed the porch of the church to be used for the first part of the rite. Some of the earliest fonts from the Middle Ages are of a tub form in lead; even earlier ones apparently were of wood. Gradually these were replaced by stone fonts, the chief characteristic of which was that they were large enough for the immersion of the candidate (by now almost always an infant). "Some 2 feet in diameter and 1 foot in depth was the average inside size of the bowl, with the tendency for the measurements to be greater rather than less."[2] This allowed ample room for immersion of newly-born babies. Baptism of babies would have been in the nude. Frequently, wooden covers were added to fonts to prevent theft of water for superstitious purposes. Octagonal fonts were common in the later Middle Ages, often with the seven sacraments and a crucifix on the sides; earlier ones often depicted the devil being crushed beneath the font.

What was in the minds of those parents who rushed their child to the font during its first days? Baptism was seen largely in terms of forgiveness of sin, at this stage in life consisting in the guilt of original sin. In the year 1439, the *Decree for the Armenians* was issued, hoping for the union of Armenian Christians with Roman Catholicism. It is based on a treatise by Thomas Aquinas and serves as a valuable point of reference to medieval developments in thinking about what was experienced in the sacraments. It tells us in official terms: "The effect of this sacrament is the remission of all sin, original and actual and all punishment which is due for this guilt."[3] Since this is so crucial, it must always be available. "In the case of necessity, however, not only a priest but a deacon, or even a layman or a woman, indeed even a pagan or heretic is able to baptize, so long as he uses the form of the Church, and intends to do what the Church does." Confirmation is more vague; normally conferred by a bishop, it may with permission be done by a "simple priest." The effect is "that through it the Holy Spirit is given to strengthen those on whom it is given as it was given to the Apostles on the day of Pentecost, namely, that the Christian might boldly confess the name of Christ."[4]

Thus in a world where society and church were synonymous, baptism had lost much of its earlier emphasis on joining the community of faith. Much more stress was placed on the individual's own salvation although the *Decree* does mention that "through it we are made members of Christ and his body, the Church." In Europe, adults to baptize were few, as witnessed to by the fact that not until 1662 did the Church of England even have a rite for "Baptism to such as Are of Riper Years."

LIVING AND DYING CHRISTIAN

Daily Public Prayer

If initiation showed a slowly moving process of change, so too did daily public prayer, especially in the West. Monks had little direct concern with baptism but daily prayer was their vocation and they shaped its development greatly in both East and West.

In the churches of the East, no less than seven distinct traditions of daily public prayer can be recognized in this period. All survive today. There is an enormous variety in these traditions. Those of *Armenia* and the *Assyro-Chaldean* (of the old Persian Empire) have retained many of the elements of the cathedral office. Robert Taft claims that the Assyro-Chaldean Church "remains the only one in Christendom, at least as far as I know, that has retained in parish worship the daily celebration of the integral cathedral cursus,"[5] namely morning prayer, evening prayer, and the vigil of feasts. The *West Syrian* and *Maronite* traditions, reaching from Syria to India, have fused elements of both cathedral and monastic offices. At the other extreme is the *Coptic* tradition in Egypt which "has retained the purest monastic form." Further south, the *Ethiopic* tradition has maintained both cathedral and monastic patterns of prayer on a daily basis in monastic communities and on the eve of eucharistic celebrations in parishes.

Most widespread is the *Byzantine* tradition, itself a fusion of many elements. It reflects usage in Constantinople which, after the city was sacked by western Christians in 1204, gave up a cathedral pattern for a monastic one, accompanied by a transfusion of hymnic poetry. Contrasting themes of darkness and light alternate both in words and ceremonial. Compared to western use, the Byzantine office seems much more ecstatic and joyful and that may account for its widespread use from Greece northward and eastward across the Balkans, Ukraine, and Russia.

The West was to see its own distinctive changes including the disappearance of the cathedral office as an option. Instead, we have what Taft calls the "monasticization" of daily public prayer. Daily prayer as practiced by monks shaped that offered in parish churches everywhere. After the eleventh century, even parish churches sprouted long monastic chancels with stalls on either side of a central aisle, the ideal monastic form for antiphonal chanting of the psalter. And parish clergy were expected to worship together "in choir" whenever possible, just as if they all were monks. In deploring the late medieval development of private recitation of the daily office, Pierre Salmon speaks glowingly of "the sublime reality that had existed for ten centuries: [before the sixteenth] the prayer celebrated officially and publicly at the same hours in all the churches of one and the same diocese, and, in parallel fashion, in all the dioceses."[6]

Salmon writes as a monk and ignores the fact that, except for religious and clergy, early in the Middle Ages the daily office ceased to function in the daily routine of ordinary people. The office remained in Latin which few of them understood. They could stand in the nave and listen or engage in their own devotions but except for matins before mass and Sunday vespers the daily office held few attractions for them. Prayer had become a professional responsibility, done *for* the people *by* monks and clerics.

For the monks, the daily and night offices were an ideal reflection of their life style devoted to contemplation and reflection. The day and night were divided by the eight offices at stated intervals: vespers, compline, matins, lauds, prime, terce, sext, and none. In less strict communities, some might be bunched together or said in advance by "anticipation." It meant immersion in the psalter which was said through (at least in theory) once a week. To this were added various canticles, office hymns, legends from the lives of saints, readings from patristic sermons, lessons from both Old and New Testaments, prayers, responses, and the Apostle's Creed.

Ideally the daily office was sung and plainsong (Gregorian chant) became the perfect vehicle for a dispassionate and meditative recital. Psalms might be sung responsorally or with antiphons (a select verse) at the beginning and end. The long chancels with choir stalls facing each other across the central aisle dominated monastic buildings and were functionally designed for the office.

In the course of time, the Office of the Blessed Virgin Mary and the Office of the Dead, consisting of more psalms and prayers, were tacked onto the traditional or canonical hours. Late in the Middle Ages, these offices were translated into the vernacular for devout lay people along with certain penitential psalms. These appeared as main components of various unofficial Primers, books for lay devotions, and helped to prepare the way for worship in the Reformation era.

The weekly monastic schedule began increasingly to conflict with the sanctoral cycle of commemorations of saints. For various saints, specific psalms and prayers not in the normal sequence were indicated. As time passed and the calendar filled up with more and more commemorations, the weekly recital of the psalter became more and more jeopardized. With the office becoming more complex, one thing gave way and that was the systematic reading of scripture. What was originally referred to as the chapter often became merely a single verse. So complicated had the whole scheme become that Cranmer remembered that often it took longer "to find out what should be read, than to read it when it was found out."

The advent of the mendicant friars in the thirteenth century brought a major revolution in the office. Monks were stable and not supposed to travel so they could sing the office together in choir. But the new forms of ministry practiced by Franciscans and Dominicans meant constant travel. Although they did not invent the breviary, i.e., all the books (psalter, antiphonary, martyrology, homiliary, collector, etc.) used by different people in the worship of a monastic community compressed into a single book, the mendicants made good use of the breviary since it enabled private recitation in the absence of the community. The breviary privatized what had always been a corporate and usually sung form of worship. Students at the new universities and the papal court had embraced it by the fifteenth century. Even parish clergy frequently came to prefer private recitation to prayers in choir for it allowed more time for other activities. Monastic communities retained its communal use.

The Eucharist

For lay people, the eucharist provided the most common form of public worship which they attended on Sundays and a multitude of feast days. What probably concerned them least was the texts from which the priest read, but we shall touch base with this staple of liturgical scholarship first before moving on to what the people saw and experienced in the mass.

The earliest mass books in the West were the prayers for a single mass written out in various leaflets known as *libelli*. It was inevitable that collections of these should develop, bringing together the priest's prayers for a number of Sundays and feast days.

The most important and oldest of these collections is known as the *Veronense* (formerly called the Leonine Sacramentary) which contains over three hundred sets of mass prayers, some of which may date from the time of Pope Leo I (440–461). When these collections of *libelli* were sorted out so they could be used easily in the course of a year, they were known as sacramentaries. They also included the necessary prayers for initiation and ordination as well as the presider's prayers for the hours of prayer on important feast days.

The most important sacramentaries are the *Gelasian* which may contain elements from Pope Gelasius I (492–496); and the *Gregorian,* named after Pope Gregory I (590–604). Various versions of these were in use in churches throughout the West. In the late eighth century, Charlemagne saw liturgical uniformity as a means to achieve unity in his empire. He requested an authentic Roman sacramentary from Pope Hadrian I (772–795) and received a very incomplete copy of the Gregorian about 785, which is known as the *Hadrianum.* One of Charlemagne's advisors, Benedict of Aniane (ca. 750–821) added a *Supplement* of prayers drawn from a variety of older Roman and Gallican sources currently in use. He prefaced it with a statement saying he had collected the missing liturgical materials endeavoring "to gather them like spring flowers, arrange them in a beautiful bouquet" in order that for priests "the present abundant collection will meet all their liturgical needs."[7] Although Benedict is quite clear that the Hadrianum is obligatory and the materials in the *Supplement* are optional, this distinction was soon blurred. In the tenth century, these non-Roman materials from northern Europe found their way back to Rome and can still be found in Roman Catholic and Protestant eucharistic rites today.

Another type of book was the *ordo* or collection of ceremonial directives on how to perform a service. Collections of these *ordines,* many originating in Rome, began to circulate north of the Alps and became treated as authoritative documents on how to perform various services. Most of these ordines were notes taken by pilgrims of things they had seen done in Rome itself, frequently papal services. Many of these ordines of the eighth and ninth centuries fitted well into the programs of Charlemagne and his father Pepin III to reform worship in France and Germany on the model of Roman use. The incentives for such efforts at unity came from north of the Alps, not from Rome itself. But uniformity was never achieved in either liturgical texts or rubrics and a variety of local, frequently diocesan, uses, perhaps as many as two hundred, flourished in Europe until the end of this period.

For the lay person attending mass faithfully every Sunday and holy day, the trajectory of this whole period was that of mass becoming more and more remote. A good example of this was the altar-table itself receding further and further from view until it finally became lodged firmly against the east wall of the church. The bishop or priest who formerly had faced the people across the altar-table now turned his back on them. From the twelfth century on, the chief action they could glimpse through the rood-screen that separated nave from chancel was the elevation when the priest raised the consecrated host above his head. Seeing this moment came to be the high point of the mass and people were known to shout "Heave it higher sir priest" if they could not see and adore.

But not only in physical proximity did the mass grow remote. The mass remained entirely in Latin and this did not vanish for Roman Catholics until 1967. And the central prayer of thanksgiving (the canon) was said in a low voice that would have prevented even Latin speakers from hearing. A very telling comment came in a letter from Stephen Gardiner, the Catholic bishop of Winchester, England, in 1547: "The people in the church took small heed what the priest and the clerks did in the chancel. . . . And therefore it was never meant that the people should indeed hear the Matins or hear the Mass, but be present there and pray themselves in silence; with common credit to the priests and clerks, that although they hear not a distinct sound to know what they say, yet to judge that they for their part were and be well occupied, and in prayer, and so should they be."[8]

A late medieval development rendered even the congregation superfluous when the priest was saying a "private" mass. As people left endowments after their death, a corps of priests grew up to say mass for the repose of the souls of the dead. Guilds could pay mass stipends for deceased members.

THE EUCHARIST

First three centuries	Fourth to sixth centuries	Medieval
greeting		
		Psalm 43
		confiteor
	introit	
	(litany), *Kyrie* response	
	Gloria in excelsis	
	collect	
(Old Testament lections)		
(psalm)		
Epistle		
(psalm)	gradual, alleluia, tract	(sequence)
Gospel		
Sermon		
		Nicene Creed
(dismissal of catechumens)		
(prayer of the faithful)		
(kiss of peace)		
offertory		
		offertory prayers and ceremonies
	prayer over the gifts	
eucharistic prayer	preface, *sanctus*, inter- cessions	
	Lord's Prayer	
	kiss of peace	
fraction		*Agnus Dei* commixture priest's prayers "Lord, I am not worthy."
giving bread and wine	communion song	
		silent prayer ablutions
	prayer after communion	
	blessing with dismissal	
		(last gospel) (concluding prayers)

DIAGRAM 3

Other instances of progressive remoteness include the disinclination to receive from the chalice which became common in the twelfth century for fear of spilling the blood of Christ. Previously, people might drink through a straw (*fistula*) or by dipping the bread in the chalice (intinction). For various reasons, most people ceased receiving communion frequently. Many devout people felt four times a year (Christmas, Easter, Pentecost, and the patronal festival of their parish church) was sufficient and a whole series of councils and synods fussed at the populace for neglecting to receive at least yearly at Easter.

So how did the people remain "well occupied" during mass? One theory is that participation came to be understood largely in visual terms.[9] We incline to equate participation today with hearing, understanding, and responding. For medieval people, there were actions such as standing up for the gospel, kneeling at the consecration, and looking at the elevation, all of which gave some connection to what the priest was doing. But there was plenty to see in the nave itself from the painting of the last judgment over the chancel arch, to saints painted on the walls and glazed in the windows, to sculptured images in wood and stone everywhere, to the images of the deceased on the floor beneath their feet. The whole building was a textbook of saints of the past and warnings of the future.

Beside visual participation, there were devotions which could occupy them during mass. In the late Middle Ages, these included the rosary and the prayers Bishop Gardiner mentioned. The most characteristic medieval eucharistic piety was reflected in these devotions, a penitential piety. We have offended a righteous God and must beg for mercy for we are not worthy. Making penance necessary to receiving communion, the ever-present fear of death and its horrors for the ungodly, and a great deal of moralistic preaching all contributed to the cultivation of a very penitential eucharistic piety. This provided the dominant piety for the Protestant Reformation and is still very much alive and well today. It is no accident that the chief additions to medieval mass texts are the so-called apologies, prayers asking God's forgiveness or expressing our unworthiness to minister. An introspective and subjective piety, dwelling on the sins of the individual became characteristic of western eucharistic piety and distinguished it from the eastern emphasis on adoration and awe before God.

It took a long time for Christians to find words for what they experienced in the mass. The ninth century saw the articulation of two views which have dogged eucharistic theology right up to the present. Two monks from the same Abbey, Corbie in northern France, spoke of how Christians interpreted the mass. Both agreed that it was the reality of Christ but Ratramnus (ca. 800–868) said it was experienced in a symbolic or metaphoric way while Paschasius Radbertus (ca. 785–860) argued that Christians ate the very flesh of Christ and drank his blood.[10] By the eleventh century, Berengarius (ca. 999–1088) found that the boundaries of faith no longer included the symbolic view (although Augustine had accommodated both) and Lanfranc (ca. 1005–1089) forced him to recant and to assert that the teeth of the believer actually crushed the body of Christ.

In the twelfth century, the West finally found the term that was to express satisfactorily for several centuries what Christians believe they experience in the eucharist, the word "transubstantiation." After over a thousand years without any term on which there was consensus, this one became normative for the West. Scholastic theologians interpreted it in terms of Aristotelian physics, a strange instance of a pagan voicing a Christian mystery. Part of the scholastic concern was to put down the popular imagination which relished stories of bleeding hosts, donkeys kneeling, Jews converted, house fires put out, and bad priests penalized by the consecrated bread. Popular piety always seemed to prefer miraculous to philosophical explanations.

Popular piety also had trouble in grasping the fine distinctions made by the theologians in speaking of the mass as sacrifice. All this tied in with the legalistic medieval interpretation of the atonement in juridical terms as a penalty Christ paid to satisfy the justice of God the Father. As Anselm argued, humans "cannot be saved without satisfaction for sin."[11] The mass became their contact with Christ's satisfaction of God's justice. Still, when the mass could be seen as a means humans offered to propitiate God, what was to stop it being offered to bring about some worthy end or some not so worthy such as the death of an enemy? Medieval councils found it necessary to forbid the latter from continuing. Such power greatly enhanced the position of priests for it gave them control over God's dispositions in this life and the next. And it also provided priests an important source of revenue in the form of mass stipends. The economic history of liturgy remains to be written.

Christian Time

We can be briefer in discussing time. As we have already seen, the contours of the liturgical week and liturgical year were mostly in place by the end of the fourth century. The Christmas and Easter cycles remain virtually unchanged even today. A few major feasts were added in the Middle Ages. Originally, All Saints' Day was celebrated in the Easter Season but an English custom of observing it on November 1 came to prevail in the West. Especially after the council of Ephesus in 431 (at which the Motherhood of God was one main issue) various Marian feasts came to dot the calendar, Ethiopia eventually having over thirty of them. Presentation and Annunciation were long seen as primarily Marian feasts and her birth (September 8) and her death or Dormition or Assumption (August 15) were all being observed in Rome by the seventh century. Two other Marian feasts eventually became popular in the West: the Visitation (July 2 in the East, May 31 in the West in recent years) and the Conception of Mary (December 8, nine months prior to September 8). The later feast, apparently, originated in England. It was stubbornly opposed by Bernard and Thomas Aquinas when it was promoted as the Immaculate Conception but prevailed largely due to the sponsorship of the Franciscans. The Feast of the Immaculate Conception did not become obligatory for Roman Catholics until 1708.

Trinity Sunday is an anomaly, commemorating a doctrine rather than a person or event. It came into prominence in the West at the beginning of the second millennium. Originally, it was celebrated at either end of the Season after Pentecost but in the fourteenth century it was permanently fixed at the Sunday after Pentecost. Also confined to the West was the observance of Corpus Christi which duplicates some elements of Maundy Thursday and occurs on the Thursday after Trinity Sunday. The Feast of Corpus Christi was imposed on the West in the thirteenth century and in the late Middle Ages became an occasion for processions and week-long festivals.

The other chief medieval contribution came in the form of the ever-proliferating cult of the saints. At first, only local martyrs and confessors plus those of Rome were observed. But gradually local ascetics, virgins, bishops, and other heroic Christians came to be venerated at the location of their burial and on the anniversary of their heavenly birthday. Beginning in the fifth century, relics were transported and became the center of much medieval piety. (People were even canonized for successful thefts of relics; St. Andrew's relics got to Scotland by means of a theft.) Pilgrimages to visit holy places and things such as the holy house at Walsingham or the tomb of Thomas Becket at Canterbury became a major part of medieval piety.

The saints were remembered on their feasts. These observances may have originated in sermons preached locally on the anniversary of their death. Gradually, appropriate prayers and readings were added. In the eighth century, Bede composed a systematic martyrology listing the saints on their feast day. Local churches celebrated their own saints, many of whom were unknown elsewhere. Not until the late twelfth century, however, did it become mandatory for Rome to approve the canonization of saints. In the eastern churches, canonization is a rare process.

The cult of saints wreaked havoc on the orderly recital of the daily office and mass. As saints accumulated over the centuries, more and more days were devoted to their memorials and the calendar became increasingly complicated.

Pastoral Rites

The medieval period saw significant changes in the pastoral rites as each underwent its own peculiar development. The chief common factor was increased clericalization as clergy became more and more essential. Priests came to acquire power and control over both penance and healing. Baptisms in emergencies could be performed by lay people (more commonly by midwives than men) and only lay people in the West could contract matrimony. At most, a lay person could perform one and a half sacraments (marriage requiring two lay persons). Bishops were everywhere necessary for ordination and usually for confirmation in the West.

1. Reconciliation. Perhaps the most drastic shifts come in penance. As we have seen, in the early period penance was rare and for only really serious sinners. The impetus for change seems to have come from the Irish church which had, in the fifth and sixth centuries, developed peculiar institutions. One of these was the practice of confession to a holy person, man or woman. Many, but not all, of these happened to be monastics. In the course of time, they began to write guidelines known as penitentials. The *Penitential of Finnan* (about 540) mandates of anyone who starts a violent quarrel "if he is a layman, he shall do penance for a week, since he is a man of this world and his guilt is lighter in this world and his reward less in the world to come."[12]

Gradually, as Irish missionaries spread through much of northern Europe, these traditions of so-called tariff penance, i.e., with penalties attached, came to prevail. An important difference ensued, the person hearing confession and granting absolution came always to be a priest, ordination not holiness becoming the qualifying criterion. What had been a relatively rare occurrence, came to be mandatory for all; what had been a once in a lifetime affair came to be annual at least. A fatal linkage between worthiness and the eucharist was made when the Fourth Lateran Council decreed in 1215 that annual penance was a prerequisite to receiving communion.

The details of penance were progressively worked out in the West. In the twelfth century, Peter Lombard (ca. 1100–1160) tells us that "by penance not only once, but often, we rise from our sins, and that true penance may be done repeatedly."[13] He lays out "three steps to be observed, that is compunction of the heart [contrition or sorrow], confession of the mouth, satisfaction in deed."[14] The fifteenth-century *Decree for the Armenians* sees the effect of penance in an individualistic way as "the absolution from sins" pronounced by a priest when he says "I absolve you," but makes no mention of reconciliation to the community.

2. Healing. The changes in anointing of the sick were no less drastic. From a sacrament administered by lay people with oil blessed by a bishop with the express purpose of healing, it became entirely clericalized and completely associated with the dying. It even acquired a new name, "extreme unction," first used by Peter Lombard about 1150. The attendance of a priest at the bedside of a dying person became necessary for a safe departure. Extreme unction came to be linked to a final confession and last communion (*viaticum*). In the popular mind, extreme unction became a form of insurance against the fires of hell. Sins that baptism and penance had left untouched during a lifetime could be removed by extreme unction.

It became a very effective form of penance instead of healing. Aquinas tells us "that the principal effect of this sacrament is the remission of sin as to its remnants, and consequently, even as to its guilt."[15] The "sickness of sin" became the focus rather than the sickness of the body. Indeed, if one did recover after extreme unction, he or she was treated as if living on borrowed time. Well could the eastern churches argue that the West had changed the sacrament of healing into the sacrament of dying.

3. *Christian Marriage.* The sacrament of marriage developed in quite different ways. Since most medieval theologians were celibates, many were less than positive about marriage although it had one important end: it produced more theologians and priests. It usually came last in the list of sacraments and was seen as at least having the merits of being a restraint on lust and a source of reproduction. Unlike the others, it was instituted before the fall of Adam and Eve as a duty before and as a remedy for sin after. But it had to be reckoned a sacrament nevertheless since a mistranslation of Ephesians 5:32 had turned *mystérion* into *sacramentum* and who could argue with scripture?

The practice of marriage is that of ever increasing proximity to church and altar-table. Throughout most of the first millennium, Christians, like everyone else, were married at home. Gradually, under the influence of ancient Roman Law, the concept of marriage as a contract came to be dominant. This led to marriages being contracted at the porch of the church where legal contracts were ratified in the sight of God and the community. Chaucer's fourteenth-century Wife of Bath had had five husbands "at the church door" and was looking for number six. As order increasingly prevailed out of chaos, legal documents became necessary to establish inheritances and legitimate births. Since the only person in most villages who could read and write was the priest, he became necessary to provide a record. Late in the Middle Ages, the whole process edged inside the church where a nuptial mass could be celebrated and the couple blessed during mass. In Luther's Saxony, the whole rite still had not moved inside the church by 1529; in England it had by 1549.

The wedding vows had to be pronounced in public, freely and mutually, and canon law devoted detailed attention to ensuring regularity in weddings. Of necessity the vows were the earliest liturgical fragment to be in the vernacular. Those from a fourteenth-century *Manual* manuscript still sound quite familiar: "Here I take you [name] to my wedded wife, to hold and to have at bed and at board, for fairer for [fouler], for better for worse, in sickness and in health, till death us do part, if holy Church it will ordain, and thereto I plight you my troth."[16]

Eastern churches saw rather different theological and liturgical developments. The priest was considered the minister of the sacrament, hence divorce and remarriage were not prohibited. The ceremony included a procession around a table in the nave and the crowning of husband and wife as rulers over a new kingdom, the Christian home as eschatological sign of the Kingdom of God based on love.

4. Christian Burial. Rites of Christian burial held an important place in medieval piety, especially because of the significance of prayer for the dead. Indeed, the Third Lateran Council in 1179 spoke of the burial of a Christian as a sacrament. Burial remained the normal form of disposal, partly because of the example of the Lord and partly because of the resurrection of the body. A great deal of medieval piety focused on death; it was recalled in the painting of the last judgment in most parish churches and in the office of the dead.

Unlike the early churches where the focus was on hope, the keynote came to be that of fear. The terrors of death for the ungodly were stressed in such songs as the thirteenth-century *Dies Irae* (Day of Wrath) sung at funerals. Vivid images reminded the living of the torments of the damned and invoked dread of judgment day: "Rescue me from fires undying; /With thy favored sheep, O place me; /Nor among the goats abase me; /but to thy right hand upraise me./ While the wicked are confounded,/ Doomed to flames of woe unbounded./ Call me: with thy saints surrounded."[17]

Ordinary people were buried simply in shrouds and after thirty years, like Hamlet's Yorick, could be dug up to be replaced. Only the wealthy could afford coffins and monuments. A requiem mass might be said after the priest met the body at the gate of the church yard (lych gate) and proceeded to the grave for the burial. Even here the monastic custom of no one dying unattended in the community and processions with psalms had their influence on death in the village. Processions from home to church to cemetery mark the course of this last rite of passage.

LIVING TOGETHER IN COMMUNITY

Leadership

The life of the Christian community underwent major changes in both East and West. Nowhere was this more apparent than in leadership roles. The net result was the development of an ecclesiastical caste system making the ordained clergy essential to the salvation of ordinary people. Monks (most of whom were not ordained) and other religious operated on a separate, we might say express, track to heaven. Bishops and priests were essential to confecting five sacraments; without them these sacraments simply were not available. In the East, clergy could receive the sacrament of matrimony before ordination; bishops were chosen from the celibate monks.

Charismatics were no longer recognized in any formal way. Instead there was a system of progression through orders that were frankly ranked from lower to higher. Hierarchialism was in full flower.

In the West, one began with the minor orders: porter, reader, psalmist (in Gaul), exorcist, and acolyte. A crucial step came before "advancing" to major orders when candidates to become a subdeacon renounced marriage. Then followed the orders of deacon (which might mean a lifetime ministry in the East but from the late Middle Ages was only transitory in the West) and priesthood. A curious double tradition survives even today. Peter Lombard, in the twelfth century, tells us that bishops and priests are of the same order. They are distinguished "not of orders, but of dignities or of offices. Bishop is the name both of a dignity and of an office"[18] and Roman Catholic bishops were consecrated rather than ordained until 1968 (the Methodist position). But another tradition saw bishops as a separate order (the Anglican position).

Since several of the minor orders (porter and exorcist) and the subdiaconate disappeared in 1972, it is easily forgotten that clergy in minor orders played an important role in parish churches and joined in the daily office so that it was far from a solo performance. In other words, there was a variety of ministries and only major orders involved celibacy.

The simpler ordination rites of the early Christian centuries focused on the laying on of hands with invocation of the Holy Spirit for the requisite gifts of ministry for each order. In the tenth century, German sources led to the compilation of new ordination rites, built upon the earlier rites but with an addition of ceremonies: anointing of a priest's hands, putting on vestments, and especially the handing over of symbolic instruments (key for porter, book for reader, chalice and paten for priests). A new book for use by bishops alone appeared, the pontifical, showing that he was no longer thought of as a local chief pastor. The most important service book of this type is known as the *Romano-Germanic Pontifical*. It originated in Germany in the tenth century around 950, was soon brought to Rome and, owing to current liturgical decadence there, soon became domesticated as the typical Roman book. From there, its spread over all of Europe was inevitable, conflating as it did earlier practices and medieval ceremonial. Late medieval sources such as the *Decree for the Armenians* identify the handing over of instruments as the essential matter for ordinations. At any rate, this confusion of riches became the basis for the pontifical which Bishop William Durandus (1230–1296), nominally of Mende in southern France, produced in the late thirteenth century and the ancestor of that edited by A. P. Piccolomini and John Burchard in 1485.

Preaching

The preaching of the gospel has always been one of the chief functions of the ordained, indeed Vatican II called it the most important work of a priest. The Middle Ages gives evidence of a series of revivals in the amount and quality of preaching. Of first importance was the development of standard mass lectionaries for the various churches of East and West. These became widely available in the sixth century but differ in Spain or Milan or Rome, many having an Old Testament lesson, a Pauline epistle, and a gospel. With the growing fixity of pericopes, the sermon came to relate to the propers of each occasion. Brilioth says that "the basic pattern of the sermon during the Middle Ages was liturgical. Within the solemn context of the mass the priest was to exegete the pericope for the day. This was one of the most significant contributions of the Middle Ages to the development of preaching."[19]

Charlemagne was quick to recognize the importance of preaching for his imperial and liturgical reforms and the Carolingian renaissance saw a revival of preaching. Alcuin (ca. 735–804) and others produced volumes of sample sermons (postils) and various homiletic helps. Books of illustrations, often from the lives of the saints, were a crutch for limping preachers then as today. The twelfth century saw preaching used as the chief means of promoting crusades as clergy from popes down to village priests found it a fervent means of enlisting support. The advent of the mendicants in the thirteenth century gave a fresh boost to preaching. Their work probably both discouraged parish clergy from competing and gave them incentive to preach more diligently. The mendicants frequently built large hall churches designed specifically for preaching. It is no accident that pews begin to appear in churches for the first time a century after the mendicants began preaching all over Europe.

Much medieval preaching was exegetical, moving on to practical applications. For better or worse, several methods of exegesis were used: literal, moral, allegorical, and anagogical. All too often the last provided an easy way to handle difficult texts by raising them to lofty significance no matter what the writer had intended. The simplest word could be contorted to have many meanings. Just imagine what one could do with the term Jerusalem alone! But then, the Middle Ages has no monopoly on misuse of scripture. Scholasticism gave fresh incentive to more theologically- and biblically-informed preaching.

Late in the Middle Ages, conscientious pastors experimented with an unofficial addendum to the Sunday mass, a service known as prone. This included in the vernacular commonly known items such as "Hail, Mary" and the Lord's Prayer, a prayer of confession, and a sermon. All this usually came before the Latin mass (or Evening Vespers) began but it provided a pattern upon which sixteenth-century reformers, Zwingli in particular, built.

There was, of course, a long succession of prophetic preachers of immense religious and social importance, calling for reforms in church and society. The fact that so many sermons have survived, sermons by men such as Bernard of Clairvaux, Bishop Robert Grosseteste of Lincoln, John Wyclif, and last but not least, Girolamo Savonarola, shows the high esteem medieval churches had of preaching.[20]

Church Music

Music played a central role in medieval worship. There was both the practical use of it in singing services but also a deeper theoretical fascination. Under this theoretical turn lies Augustine's treatise *De Musica* in which he defined music as "the art of the well-ordered." He associates music with mathematics in the sense of being properly proportioned and in harmony, a sense it shares with the whole universe. Numerical relationships can lead us beyond themselves, even to God. It is not surprising that medieval architects took seriously what Augustine had to say about music and endeavored to build with harmonious proportions.

Music played an important place in both monastery and parish but the monks set the style in music as in so much else. Plainsong was ideally suited to the contemplative singing of the psalter and it had the quality of uniting the community of men or women by singing together in unison. But nothing stands still. Toward the end of our period various forms of polyphonic singing became available in both secular and religious life. These new forms had different voices singing different parts and sometimes different words all simultaneously. Such practices may have been an unconscious reflection of the growing individualism of late medieval society but polyphony certainly was a radical shift from the chant with its single, uncluttered melody.

Throughout this period, new office hymns (concluding with a doxological stanza) were written for the daily office and to commemorate new saints as they were added to the calendar. A luxuriant growth of sequences (or gradual hymns) grew up to be sung at mass. These were in Latin and were virtually exterminated in 1570 but left behind a great heritage of liturgical poetry, some of which was translated by Victorian hymn writers. In addition, there was a thousand-year tradition in Poland of vernacular hymnody in which layfolk might engage themselves while the priest went about his business at the altar-table.

Church Architecture

We have not been able to avoid entirely speaking of church architecture and in a way it sums up all the developments of this period. Over the course of nine centuries, churches in the West moved from a simple two-cell structure to a complicated building with various spaces allotted to differing liturgical functions. The outer porch provided space for parts of weddings and baptisms. Even the churchyard, usually on the south side since the north belonged to the devil (or at least Norsemen), was sacred space. Once inside the door, all was numinous space. Almost all medieval churches have been swept clean over the last few centuries and are devoid of most of the treasures with which piety endowed them. Only fragments remain of space that was adorned from rafters or vaults to the tiles on the floor.

The nave was the place for people and was used for a vast variety of community fairs and markets. Our sharp distinction of sacred and secular was unknown.[21] Beginning in the fourteenth century, a revolution occurred in many parish churches. The congregation literally sat down on the job as pews were introduced. The congregation, once mobile and able to go where preaching was best heard or the mass best seen, became static. In eastern churches, this never happened except where they have been corrupted by western influence in recent years. A seated congregation may have been the most significant change in Christian worship since Constantine.

Portions of the aisles might be partitioned off for chapels where mass would be said for the repose of illustrious dead or the common sort who had formed a guild for this purpose. There would also be altar-tables at the roodscreen that separated the people's church from the clergy's. The chancel had grown enormously, depending on the income of the living, and sometimes was two-thirds the length of the nave. Here clergy sang the daily office in their choir stalls. Beyond stood the sanctuary with the high altar-table, clergy seats, and Easter sepulcher. All in all, it was a complex building by the end of the Middle Ages with each space having a specific liturgical function.

The history of the eastern churches is somewhat different. The basic form that evolved tended to be a central type building, often under a dome. At one end was the apse where a single altar-table stood in holy space protected by an icon screen (iconostasis) and doors. A narthex formed the opposite end of the building as gathering space. Eastern churches contrasted vividly with the longitudinal churches of the West where the axis was horizontal. From around 725 to 842, the East was beset with the iconoclastic controversy over the role of icons in worship. After more than a century of trauma, the role of icons was upheld and, in two-dimensional form, they again became an important part of Orthodox piety.

In the West, the earlier Romanesque buildings with immensely heavy masonry walls, punctuated by round-headed arches and vaults were eventually replaced by the gothic, newly invented in twelfth century France. Abbot Suger of St. Denis in Paris saw mystical meanings in the new style he built and dedicated in 1140: "Bright is the noble work; but being nobly bright, the work/ Should brighten the minds, so that they may travel, through the true lights,/ To the True Light where Christ is the true door. . . . The dull mind rises to truth through that which is material."[22]

What he built was based on sacred geometry in which the proportions had spiritual values. Gothic opened up immense possibilities for building churches in which light was the key material and heavy stone supported vaults and roofs high overhead. At its best, the aesthetic appeal of gothic has never been equaled. We have come a long way from the tiny churches of the first missionaries to northern Europe.

FOR FURTHER READING

Chadwick, Henry and G. R. Evans. *Atlas of the Christian Church.* New York: Facts on File Publications, 1987.

Petry, Ray C. *A History of Christianity: Readings in the History of the Early and Medieval Church.* Englewood Cliffs, N.J.: Prentice-Hall, 1962.

Taft, Robert. *The Liturgy of the Hours in East and West.* Collegeville: Liturgical Press, 1986.

Van Dijk, S. J. P., and J. Hazelden Walker. *The Origins of the Modern Roman Liturgy.* London: Darton, Longman, and Todd, 1960.

Vogel, Cyrille. *Medieval Liturgy: An Introduction to the Sources.* Translated and revised by William Storey and Niels Rasmussen. Washington: Pastoral Press, 1986.

CHAPTER IV

Worship in the Churches of the Reformation Period

The dominant event in western Christianity during the sixteenth and seventeenth centuries was the division of the western churches by the Reformation. The period 1500–1700 begins with all the churches of the West liturgically loosely connected to Rome; by the end of this period no less than six distinct Protestant liturgical traditions were firmly established and Rome had asserted unprecedented control over worship in the Roman Catholic Tradition. All seven traditions ultimately derive from the late medieval churches of the West although some are secondary or even tertiary in derivation.

Our procedure will be to examine these seven traditions on the chief elements of worship in terms of their conservatism or radicalism with regard to the late medieval heritage. Each tradition is most easily distinguished primarily in terms of how much it retained or discarded from a common inheritance. All shared the same source but some esteemed it more highly than others. Everyone was nearly oblivious to other possibilities—early Christian, eastern churches—so that the late medieval options determined most decisions made about worship in the reformation period. Thus the usual choice was in terms of a late medieval possibility: take it, leave it, or modify it.

We shall be looking at the period from 1500 to 1700 or from the eve of the Reformation to the eve of the Enlightenment. The Enlightenment, as we shall see in the next chapter, proves just as great a shift in human consciousness and piety as does the Reformation. By comparison, much of the Reformation era in worship is simply an extension of medieval mentalities. John Calvin, for example, has much more in common with late medieval Christians than with his nineteenth-century descendant, Charles G. Finney.

An important characteristic of the Reformation period is the richness and variety of possibilities that develop in worship. This richness consists in diversity and ability to serve a wide variety of peoples. Nor was change limited to Protestant traditions; baroque Catholicism saw entirely new types of piety, architecture, and music as worship evolved to meet changes in people. And even the Orthodox churches were not left untouched by social change. We shall explore these parallel paths in their respective efforts to express the worship of God in terms relevant to a variety of peoples.

THE WORLD OF THE REFORMATION PERIOD

The most obvious change in this period for Christianity was the explosion to a worldwide faith, encompassing the globe. The end of the Middle Ages had been marked by loss of territory, especially Turkey and Greece to Islam, most graphically illustrated by the fall of Constantinople in 1453. Not only did this period mark the colonization of major portions of the Americas by Europeans but missionaries circled the globe. In this period, they were mostly Roman Catholics. They had made two million converts in the Philippines by 1620. Dioceses were established in most of South America, East Africa, and much of the Far East.

The same period saw development of new national consciousness on the level of new nation states. Some, such as England and the Scandinavian states, opted for the nationalization of churches; others, such as France, evolved a form of royal Catholicism. People everywhere were emphasizing what made them separate and distinct from other nations. As the scale of nation states increased, this brought fresh problems for conformity within countries and triggered various rebellions on the basis of worship.

An important shift in the human consciousness occurred as a result of the invention of printing around 1450. The Gutenberg revolution brought an entirely new way to pass on information on a mass level. Reading had been for the elite; the development of the book as the first mass-produced item in history meant that reading could belong to everyone. In 1450, a *Book of Common Prayer* would have been an oxymoron; a century later it was a reality. The impact for worship was tremendous. For many people, much ceremonial in worship simply became redundant because they now could experience the same realities serially through the spoken or read word. The Reformation could never have spread without the work of the publicists who took new ideas and immediately scattered them over a whole continent.

Commerce played a big role in liturgical development. The new commercial possibilities led to the growth of larger and larger cities. Usually, receptivity to new patterns of worship was more pronounced in urban areas than in country districts. Frequently, it was the new urbanized and educated classes that pressed most ardently for liturgical reform. Boston was settled to be a "city set on a hill" for all the world to see what true Reformation of worship meant. New social developments led to new worship needs.

We shall characterize briefly the liturgical traditions that exploded with amazing rapidity in the West during this period. In many ways, the Roman Catholic Tradition remained the most firmly committed to late medieval ways of worship, especially since it was often forced into a defensive position. But it was by no means stagnant, and major reforms, some deliberate, others not, occurred during this period. A pivotal change was the issuance, for the first time in history of revised service books for mandatory use everywhere save for a few venerable exceptions. Most of these new books were based on local uses in Rome itself. They include the *Roman Breviary* (1568), the *Roman Missal* (1570), the *Roman Martyrology* (1584), the *Roman Pontifical* (1596), the *Caeremoniale Episcoporum* (1600), and the *Roman Ritual* (1614).

THE PROTESTANT TRADITIONS OF WORSHIP

	Left-wing	*Central*	*Right-wing*
16th century	Anabaptist	Reformed	Anglican Lutheran
17th century	Quaker Puritan		
18th century		Methodist	
19th century	Frontier		
20th century	Pentecostal		

——————— DIAGRAM 4 ———————

The Protestant Reformation began with Martin Luther (1483–1546) and his protests against abuses in the churches of Saxony. His most significant sacramental writing was *The Babylonian Captivity of the Church* (1520) which underlies all subsequent Protestant sacramental theology. Luther was essentially conservative, feeling "the service now in common use everywhere goes back to genuine Christian beginnings."[1] He was unwilling to disturb the faithful by radical innovations. Still, he eventually published a reformed mass in 1523 (in Latin) and in 1526 (in German). Luther made notable contributions as the father of Protestant preaching and in church music. In many ways, the *Lutheran Tradition* remained the most conservative with regard to the late medieval heritage.

Much of Luther's restraint was absent in his contemporary, Ulrich Zwingli (1484–1531) of Zurich, who was willing to go much further both in liturgical forms and sacramental theology. Martin Bucer (1491–1551) of Strasbourg made further contributions to the *Reformed Tradition* but it was John Calvin (1509–1564) who gave this Tradition its definitive form. Worship tended to be most cerebral and didactic in its moral earnestness. John Knox (ca. 1505–1572) took many of these forms of worship to Scotland.

Even more radical was the *Anabaptist Tradition*, launched by a variety of reformers in Switzerland by 1525 and soon reaching

Austria and the Netherlands. Its most drastic form was refusal to acknowledge the reality of infant baptism. But it also evolved an ideal of a pure church uncompromised by support from the civil state. The Anabaptists brought a new freedom in worship forms and produced a generation of martyrs, commemorated in hymnody and martyrologies.

The *Anglican Tradition*, found in the Church of England and English colonies, tried for a middle of the road approach, conserving much of the past in outward forms but transforming much in theological interpretations. Its forms could be characterized as "not distant" from medieval forms yet the underlying sacramental theology reflected not Calvin's relatively conservative position but Zwingli's more radical. The chief monuments in this period are the *Book of Common Prayer* of 1549 and the more radical 1552 edition. Subsequent changes were introduced in 1559, 1604, and 1662.

Many English Christians found these reforms insufficient and the English Puritans sought to reform the Church of England solely on the basis of what God had prescribed in Scripture. If God's will was explicit on ethics, the *Puritan Tradition* argued, it was no less so on how God was to be served in worship. For fifteen years (1645–1660) the *Book of Common Prayer* was abolished while the Puritans controlled the national church. Much traditional ceremonial was proscribed, worship focused heavily on preaching, and a loose national uniformity was enforced on the basis of the *Westminster Directory* (1645).

During the period of Puritan supremacy, the most radical tradition of all, the *Quaker Tradition*, erupted. Its leader, George Fox (1624–1691), proposed a worship style devoid of set liturgies, sermons, music, clergy, and visible sacraments. It focused on corporate mysticism in which the Spirit could address the whole meeting through any person present, regardless of sex, race, or social status. This new emphasis on liturgical equality spilled over into the sphere of social justice. For the first time in history, worship and justice became linked and led to crusades against slavery, the recognition of the equality of women, and many reforms, all based on the Quaker experience of worship. In much of this, the Quakers were two centuries ahead of all other traditions.

BECOMING CHRISTIAN

The way many churches signified becoming a Christian was probably the least changed of all worship practices in this period. The more conservative (right wing) churches, i.e., Roman Catholic, Lutheran, and Anglican changed little, the moderate, i.e., Reformed, and even some of the left wing i.e. Puritans, scarcely more. The more radical traditions, the Anabaptists and Quakers, made up for this conservatism by introducing sweeping reforms. In quite different ways, they drastically altered their practice of Christian initiation.

The trajectory of medieval developments proved to be irreversible. No one in the Reformation seriously challenged the withholding of communion from baptized infants. It may seem an anomaly that those who were baptized were, in effect, immediately excommunicated until they had reached an age of reason, but this is still common. Nor did those who baptized infants seek to reconnect baptism with immediate confirmation as the eastern churches continued to do. The paschal significance of baptism had been so long forgotten that no one argued for postponement to the paschal season. In several traditions, baptism did indeed become linked to the Lord's Day but because of insistence on baptism being a public occasion, rather than dying and rising with Christ on Sunday.

Except for Anabaptists and Quakers, infant baptism remained the normal practice. As long as Christianity remained confined to Europe, there was no one else left to baptize except for occasional converts from Judaism or Islam, frequently under duress. The development of worldwide missions brought quite a different practice as a global faith found it necessary to baptize converts of all ages.

The usual medieval practice of baptizing infants by immersion (or dipping or submersion) gradually ended, not by any deliberate decision but by slow yielding to convenience. The rubrics of the

Roman Ritual of 1614 read in nineteenth-century editions: "Where on the other hand there is the custom of baptizing by immersion, and taking care it is not hurt, he carefully dips it, and with a triune immersion baptizes, saying at the same time. . . ."[2] These words (and the possibility they represent) disappear in twentieth-century editions as they probably had long before in practice. Luther's baptismal rites (1523 and 1526) both specify that the infant is dipped. His reasons are clear even if his tone sounds a bit defensive: "For baptism, as we shall hear, signifies that the old man and the sinful birth of flesh and blood are to be wholly drowned by the grace of God. We should therefore do justice to its meaning and make baptism a true and complete sign of the thing it signifies."[3]

The Anglican communion, too, gave this a priority and in rubrics still in force in the Church of England (although rarely heeded), the English prayerbooks have always commanded he "shall dip it in the water." What happened was concession to convenience and fashions. Charles Wheatly, writing in England in 1710, tells us that "many fond ladies at first, and then by degrees the common people, would persuade the Minister that their children were too tender for dipping. . . . So that in the latter times of queen Elizabeth, . . . there were but very few children dipped in the font" and indeed by his time "the child is always brought in such a dress, as shews that there is no intention that it should be dipped."[4]

In the Reformed Tradition, Calvin considered the mode of baptism indifferent and his followers usually practiced pouring (affusion). Most Reformed and Puritan fonts would have made immersion impossible in any case. The Anabaptists, too, were quite content with baptism by pouring. It was not until the seventeenth century that English Baptists of the Puritan Tradition began to insist on baptizing adults by immersion. Quakers saw no need for any outward sign of water and insisted that baptism, as a work of the Spirit, took no visible form. Robert Barclay (1648–1690), the great Quaker theologian, argued that baptism with water "was a figure, which was commanded for a time, and not to continue for ever" since "the professing of faith in Christ, and a holy life answering thereunto, is a far better badge of Christianity than any outward washing."[5]

The decline in baptism by immersion is reflected in the gradual shrinking of fonts. The massive medieval fonts gave way to smaller pedestal fonts and for the moderate traditions these often yielded to portable basins. With remarkable tenacity, Roman Catholics and Anglicans clung to having the font situated near the main entrance. By the seventeenth century, many Lutheran fonts had migrated to the front of the church where they stood next to altar-table and pulpit, uniting word and sacrament. Reformed and Puritan churches usually used a portable basin, always near the pulpit as Calvin dictated: "the stone or baptismal font is to be near the pulpit, in order that there be better hearing for the recitation of this mystery and practice of baptism."[6] Seventeenth-century Baptists tended to baptize in baptismal pools excavated in the floor or in nearby streams and lakes.

The fate of confirmation varied according to the tradition. By and large, it was recast as a graduation exercise for those of sufficient maturity to know the catechism. Roman Catholics defended the inherited pattern by asserting that confirmation was "a true and proper sacrament," more "than a kind of catechism," and that the ordinary minister is a bishop, not "any simple priest."[7] But the paucity of affirmations indicate a rather dubious heritage. The rite appeared in the *Roman Pontifical* of 1596.

Anglicanism came close to maintaining existing practice with a bishop as the only possible minister of confirmation. The prayerbook ratified the medieval postponement of confirmation by mandating that children being confirmed shall first have mastered the Creed, Lord's Prayer, and Decalogue plus the Catechism so they may "openly before the church ratify and confess the same." The bishop was to sign them with the sign of the cross and lay his hands on them. None was to be admitted to communion until after confirmation. The service provides little rationale; the prayers ask for the sending down of the Holy Spirit with its gifts (1549) or strengthening the children by the Holy Spirit and increasing its gifts (1552). Pains are taken to base this rite on "the example of the holy Apostles" but the chief purpose seems to be "to certify them (by this sign) of thy favor and gracious goodness toward them." In 1552, unction and the sign of the cross disappear. As in the Middle Ages, relatively few people were confirmed at first but under James I (1603–1625) it became common for all to receive confirmation.

Luther was quite explicit that he did not consider confirmation a sacrament because it has "no divine promise connected" nor does it save. But he was quite willing for the pastor to examine children and lay hands on them in confirmation. Zwingli simply abolished confirmation altogether. Calvin taunts the Catholics by asking why, if confirmation is so important, do so few of them receive it? Calvin advised having children profess their faith publicly: "thus, while the church looks on as a witness, he [the child] would profess the one true and sincere faith."[8] Out of this pattern grew the Puritan practice of baptized children making a public profession of faith or owning the covenant when of sufficient age. Puritans condemned Anglican confirmation as "superfluous" a frank statement of what had long been suspected in the West.

For Anabaptists and Quakers, even these changes were unnecessary. If only believers were baptized, as among Anabaptists, then the primitive unity of initiation was once again regained. Balthasar Hubmaier's baptismal rite includes a laying on of hands by the bishop which includes the words: "you shall be counted among the Christian community, as a member participating in the use of her keys, breaking bread and praying with other Christian sisters and brethren."[9] For a time, English Baptists practiced laying on of hands by the pastor at believers' baptisms. Quakers saw no more need for the outward sign of confirmation than they did for water baptism.

The most radical break with medieval practice came with the Anabaptists if we except the Quakers who discarded outward sacramental forms altogether. The Anabaptist movement began with the Swiss Brethren in Zurich although various others in Luther's own Saxony had already raised doubts about infant baptism. Inspired by Zwingli's aggressive reforming actions in Zurich, several priests from nearby towns urged him to go further and openly break with the age-old practice of infant baptism. But Zwingli, whose reforms were accomplished through the support of the city council, had reached his point of conservatism and refused to yield on this point. Despite several disputations before the city council in 1523 and 1525, the Anabaptists were not able to prevail and were hounded out of the city.

Zwingli realized, no doubt, that the influence and power of the church would be greatly diminished if it became a purely voluntary affair devoid of connection to civil government. Had he accepted the premises of the Anabaptists, his power base would have evaporated; on the other hand he might not have died on the battlefield in 1531. For the Anabaptists were concerned to establish a church of professing believers only. The ideal church was to be pure, not mixed with godly and ungodly joined in a state church. It was rather a sect of gathered Christians firmly committed to the religious life, very much like a religious order living in the world. The Hutterian Brethren with their communistic societies managed to avoid even that contagion.

The clearest sign of the pure church was that one became a member by deliberate choice, not by baptism as an infant. Zwingli put up a good defense of infant baptism as a sign that children were within the covenant community and introduced a totally new concept, that baptism was a means by which parents "dedicated" their children to God. The Anabaptists argued on two grounds: scripture and reason. One of their ablest leaders, a former priest who started reading scripture two years after his ordination, Menno Simons (1496–1561), found that the Bible made no mention of the baptism of infants. Rather, the opposite, for it said that "the one who believes and is baptized will be saved" (Mark 16:16) and it speaks of making "disciples of all nations, baptizing them" (Matt. 28:19). He concluded "we have not a single command in the Scriptures that infants are to be baptized, or that the apostles practiced it, therefore we confess with good sense that infant baptism is nothing but human invention and notion."[10] Furthermore, reason showed that "young children are without understanding and unteachable." The debate has continued for well over four centuries but arguments on either side have scarcely improved. Anabaptists saw no necessity for immersion. Their insistence on a pure church led inevitably to conflicts with Protestants and Catholics alike and resulted in many of them becoming martyrs. Hubmaier's writings about threefold baptism, the "Spirit given internally, . . . water given externally, . . . and that of blood in martyrdom"[11] was fulfilled in his own life as in many of his followers.

Most striking for average believers must have been Hubmaier's first baptisms done with a milk pail. Could anything have been more shocking to those burgers of Waldshut than to forsake the ancient stone font of his parish church in order to baptize (or rebaptize) from such an ordinary household item? This Hubmaier did for three hundred of his parishioners on Easter Day, 1525. These outward and visible changes are sure signs of major inward shifts in what becoming a Christian meant.

But most Christians of the Reformation era were confronted by far less drastic changes either inward or outward. Trent had nothing new to say for Catholics. It continued the defense of the validity of baptism even by heretics and defended infant baptism. Luther found that baptism, unlike other sacraments, had by God been "preserved in his church . . . untouched and untainted by the ordinances of men."[12] His great contribution in this instance was not in terms of theology but in terms of piety. Luther sketches out a whole new baptismal spirituality which in many ways is still ahead of us; "For as long as we live we are continually doing that which baptism signifies, that is, we die and rise again. . . . You may indeed wander away from the sign for a time, but the sign is not therefore useless . . . that which baptism signifies should swallow up your whole life, body and soul, and give it forth again at the last day, clad in the robe of glory and immortality. We are therefore never without the sign of baptism nor without the thing it signifies."[13] Luther is said to have signed himself daily while reminding himself that he was baptized. He felt life knew no greater comfort than baptism.

For both Zwingli and Calvin, baptism is connected with predestination (which Anabaptists tended to deny). It is commanded of all but effective only for the elect. Calvin had a deep understanding of the value of signs; baptism "effectively performs what it symbolizes." He staunchly defends the baptism of children of believers although children dying unbaptized are not necessarily denied salvation. Yet salvation comes through membership in the body of the elect found within, and only within, the visible church. He begins his discussion of baptism in the *Institutes* by saying: "Baptism is the sign of the initiation by which we are received into the society of the church, in order that, engrafted in Christ, we may be reckoned among God's children."[14] The theme of incorporation into the church seems to be Calvin's most important stress as over against the highly individualistic forms of late medieval piety with its primary concern for the forgiveness of sins. Zwingli, too, places his emphasis on the communal aspects of baptism but he has none of Calvin's sense of the effectiveness of baptism as a sign that removes the condemnation and punishment due sin.

The insistence on baptism as a public act carried over into the Anglican and Puritan traditions as well. For the Church of England, baptism "should not be ministered but upon Sundays and other holy days, when the most number of people may come together." This ensured that "every man present may be put in remembrance of his own profession to God in his baptism."[15] Although the 1549 prayerbook provided a form for blessing the water in the font, this disappeared in 1552. The community itself comes to function almost as part of the "matter" of baptism for it is into it that one is baptized by water.

The Quakers affirmed the importance of the Spirit-filled community but without need for any visible signs. Their rejection of traditional forms is thorough:

> All other worship, then, both praises, prayers, or preachings, which man sets about in his own will, and at his own appointment, which he can both begin and end at his pleasure, do or leave undone as he seeth meet, whether they be a prescribed form as a liturgy, &c., or prayers conceived extempore by the natural strength and facility of the mind, they are all but superstition, will-worship, and abominable idolatry in the sight of God, which are now to be denied and rejected, and separated from, in this day of spiritual arising.[16]

Baptism and the Lord's Supper may have been observed in the New Testament but that was no warrant for observing them beyond a limited time any more than there was for footwashing.

Prescribed forms were to be avoided as human inventions rather than God's intent. This did not mean that baptism was abolished but merely that it no longer required "visibles." Instead, it was "a pure and spiritual thing, to wit, the baptism of the Spirit and fire."[17] That which is signified, the Spirit, needs no outward sign but can operate entirely inwardly. Christianity is "pure and spiritual, and not carnal and ceremonial." But it is communal and those who have received the inward baptism of the Spirit (though not the outward of water) must assemble. God "causeth the inward life (which is also many times not conveyed by the outward senses,) the more to abound, when his children assemble themselves diligently together to wait upon him. . . . And as many candles lighted, and put in one place, do greatly augment the light, and make it more to shine forth, . . . each individual . . . partakes not only of the light and life raised in himself, but in all the rest."[18] This Tradition, most radical in rejecting so much of the medieval inheritance, is nevertheless as conservative as any in valuing the community and its assembling.

Changes in baptismal practice and belief are inherently changes in concepts of what the Church is. We see in the Reformation era a wide spectrum ranging from state churches where all are compelled to receive baptism at birth to sectarian churches where only the devout are considered eligible for baptism. Yet all agree that baptism places one within the Body of Christ where the Holy Spirit works.

LIVING AND DYING CHRISTIAN

The Reformation period brought about enormous changes in all aspects of Christian life and worship. This was true for those who clung to the "Old Religion" as well as the newer forms. Everyone seemed caught in a furious whirlpool of change in all that was familiar in worship.

Daily Public Prayer

Most of the attempts to reform daily public prayer were more or less directed to de-monasticizing and de-clericalizing it. The monastic orders, of course, saw no need for this but they had vanished in most Protestant lands and the center of the stage for

Roman Catholicism was now occupied by upstart new orders, spawned in the wake of the Reformation. A sign of this transformation came as new orders were organized with no obligation to say the office together. Theatines, Oratorians, Ursulines, Capuchins all sprang up in the sixteenth century not based on the old monastic orders. The climax came when the Society of Jesus was recognized in 1540 without obligation to sing the office in choir in order to be free to carry on their work in the world. These new orders soon set the fashions in church architecture and music just as the monastics once had prevailed.

Private recitation, which had been allowed as an exception for the friars engaged in traveling ministry in the thirteenth century, had been extended to students in the new universities by the following century, and gradually became common among parish clergy in the fifteenth century. Even the monks themselves were struggling with the burdensomeness of the office to which some attributed the marked decline in monastic vocations. Ignatius of Loyola, founder of the Jesuits, was a man of a new age for whom mission was primary. "Jesuit work and piety was directed *ad extra*, and Ignatius resolutely refused to legislate *anything* that would interfere with or restrict in any way the Jesuit apostolic obligation to serve where necessary. All else was subordinate to this: prayer, dress, penance—and liturgy."[19]

But the breviary itself had already been the subject of much effort at reform. The need was widely recognized; all agreed the office was too complicated because of the constant intrusions of the saints' commemorations. In 1525, Martin Bucer, a Dominican priest, inaugurated a vernacular daily public prayer for his flock in Strasbourg.[20] He limited it to morning and evening hours, removed the antiphons and responses, and emphasized continuous reading of the Bible: New Testament in the morning and Old in the evening. Many of these same ideas were to resurface a decade later in the breviary of Cardinal Quiñones.

Luther set his hand to a reform of the office in his *German Mass*, published in 1526. This included matins and vespers. He had in mind primarily use in schools and for that purpose retained Latin as well as German for some of the psalms, canticles, and lessons. A pronounced feature of all these services is the emphasis on the systematic reading of Scripture, Luther insisting on a whole chapter at each office "since the preaching and teaching of God's Word is the most important part of divine service."[21] On Sundays, there was a sermon on the epistle at matins, on the gospel at mass, and on the Old Testament lesson at vespers. This insistence on lessons and sermons is not the pattern of the early Church at all. Luther probably did not care but other Protestant leaders seriously thought they were restoring primitive practice in making scripture central to a people's office.

Luther's antagonist, Zwingli, developed a much more radical form of daily public worship at 5 a.m. and 8 p.m. in each of the Zurich churches. In addition, there was a daily service of "Prophesying" in the main church at which the congregation could comment on the preacher's handling of the text. The preachers preached fourteen times a week, a good week's work.

The Roman Catholic effort at reform began with the work of Spanish Cardinal Francisco de Quiñones (1480–1540) in 1535 and 1536. Repeating many of the reforms a decade earlier of Bucer, although still in Latin, it restored a weekly reading of the psalter, as well as dropping items such as antiphons, responses, and increased the scriptural content. He also added a preface explaining why some of the reforms had been brought about. Not many years later, many of these words were to recur in Cranmer's preface to the Prayer Book and the same ideas were recycled in his revision of the offices in the first *Book of Common Prayer* (1549). Quiñones' revision met an obvious need; it went through more than a hundred editions in thirty years.

But it was too radical for some. The Council of Trent entrusted to the papacy the reform of the breviary and a more moderate reformed one appeared in 1568. It reduced the clutter of saints' days and shortened the office somewhat. What was most radical of all was that this new *Roman Breviary* was mandated for uniform use by all Roman Catholic churches except those (such as monastic orders and a few dioceses) that could prove their books had been in use for over two centuries. Only with the advent of printing could such uniformity be imposed. But it does represent an entirely new liturgical mentality in which Rome, after a millennium and a half of liturgical laissez-faire, could do something most untraditional, insist on liturgical uniformity. In France, where the Canons and Decrees of Trent were never promulgated, new diocesan breviaries continued to appear throughout the seventeenth and eighteenth centuries until suppressed in the mid-nineteenth.

The great success story of this period is the Anglican reform of the office. Cranmer makes his principles most clear in the preface, especially the misconception that the "ancient fathers . . . so ordered the matter, that all the whole Bible (or the greatest part thereof) should be read over once in the year."[22] He proceeds to simplify the office, as had Quiñones, by cutting out "anthems, responds, invitatories, and such like things." Most important, all is in English. Much of it consists of scripture "and that in such a language and order, as is most easy and plain for the understanding." Cranmer has accepted the new technology that print brought and touts as one of the advantages of the new book that "henceforth, all the whole realm shall have but one use." The innovation of liturgical uniformity had reached Protestantism by mid-century.

By conflating portions of matins, lauds, and prime into matins or morning prayer and by mining vespers and compline for evensong or evening prayer, Cranmer made an office that was accessible to lay people. He did not realize it but his model was still monastic. So forgotten had been that ancient cathedral (or people's) office in the West that it had no impact on what Cranmer attempted. It may have been just as well; it would have derailed his chief efforts to have the psalter read through on a monthly basis, the Old Testament yearly, and most of the New Testament thrice each year.

Cranmer's service acquired a penitential preface in 1552 which is a good reflection of the late medieval piety of "miserable offenders." But otherwise, except for a few prayers, the *Te Deum*, the Apostles' or Athanasian Creeds, it is entirely scripture as the Reformation advocated. At any rate, it worked all too well and accomplished what Cranmer never anticipated by becoming the main staple of Anglican worship on Sundays as well as weekdays. For three centuries, the usual Anglican Sunday diet of worship was morning prayer, litany, ante-communion, and sermon. Is it any wonder that Puritans complained of the "longsomeness" of the service? In the seventeenth century, a magnificent tradition developed of singing the office "in quires and places where they sing," namely, cathedral and collegiate churches. In such locales, the Anglican office still exceeds any other tradition in aesthetic quality.

The Puritans and the Reformed tradition in general made an important contribution in visualizing the Christian home as a small church and carefully cultivating daily family prayers, a tradition not entirely vanished. Diane Karay Tripp has shown the presence of an immense variety of public daily services for prayer and scripture reading.[23] Even more enduring were the various manuals for daily family worship and the *Directory for Family Worship* that the Church of Scotland approved in 1647. Heads of family who refused to attend to such matters on a daily basis could be excommunicated "as being justly esteemed unworthy to communicate." Principles and guidelines provided for worship daily and faithfully. Family worship consisted of "prayer and praises, 'reading of the scriptures,' catechizing, in a plain way . . . together with godly conferences."[24]

The Eucharist

Daily public prayer might affect many people or few depending upon whether they were Anglican or Roman Catholic. But the eucharist affected all Christians except Quakers. The reforms in the eucharist were far more varied than with daily public prayer. We shall look at a variety of these reforms, moving from the most conservative attempts to the most radical. Then we shall try to estimate what these reforms meant for the worshipers themselves.

By and large, Roman Catholics were on the defensive with regard to the eucharist. In the absence of any form of daily office for the laity, the eucharist had come to serve a variety of purposes besides regular worship. These included blessing a marriage or prayer for the dead. In addition, the entire system of salvation was structured around a juridical understanding of the atonement which was mediated through the eucharist. Finances are always important; the livelihood of thousands of priests depended upon mass stipends. There were plenty of reasons for Catholicism to conserve medieval practices and theologies with regard to the mass.

Hence it is not surprising that one after another of the reforms initiated by various Protestants were disallowed by the Council of Trent: no concession of the chalice to the laity, no allowance of the vernacular, no need for communion of children, private masses to be continued, the mass to be considered a sacrifice that is propitiatory for the living and dead, reservation of the sacrament, the need "to communicate every year, at least at Easter," and the term "transubstantiation" to be retained. The canons almost read like a list of those very things Protestants had challenged. One reason for such intransigence was that some of the bishops felt any reforms would involve a loss of face and validate Protestant claims for reform. Still, the bishops did condemn those items which reflected avarice, irreverence, and superstition.[25]

All sides suffered from the absence of any serious liturgical scholarship. Some of the bishops believed that the Roman canon had been written by St. Peter and, as unlikely as that may seem today, there was nothing to prove them wrong. Given such a mind set, to tamper with the canon was unthinkable; other portions of the mass, particularly the rich medieval growth of sequences and trophes were later treated less kindly and drastically pruned. The bishops left to the Roman curia the task of liturgical revision of the missal. The result was the *Roman Missal* of 1570, like the breviary of two years before, imposed universally and irrevocably under Pius V.

The problems of liturgical texts in Latin imposed throughout the world certainly did little to help the rapidly-developing missionary movement. Latin may have made some sense to Europeans; it made none to anyone else. The most dramatic conflict of cultures came in China where Jesuit missionaries experimented with services in Mandarin and tried to accommodate something of ancestor worship. Other religious orders interfered in Rome, largely destroying the China mission.

The most moderate reform was probably that of giving the cup to the laity. After all, scripture mandated it, the eastern churches still continued it as had the West for over a thousand years, and for over a century some followers of Jan Huss (the

Calixtines) had regained it. Luther considered withholding the chalice to be the first captivity the Romanists had created for the eucharist, and his outrage at this was echoed by all Protestants. The emperor pressed the Council of Trent for the chalice for the laity and several popes concurred, but the Council of Trent held firm.

The most noticeable reform was translation into the vernacular. Here Luther by no means led the way; his first mass, *Formula Missae* of 1523 was in Latin and others produced German masses before Luther's was published in 1526.[26] In the 1530s, French masses were produced as were Swedish, Danish, and Norwegian. In the 1540's, English and Finnish versions appeared, Dutch in the 1550s, and by the last decade of the century even Icelandic. Translation was the crucial reform just as it was for Roman Catholics in the 1960s. It meant that hearing became a form of active participation for everyone. Protestant rubrics stress audibility for all services.

The question of frequency of communion was the most problematic reform. Luther intended to have lay people commune frequently but this was a radical step for people who had only done so at the very greatest festivals. Communion four times a year is not a Protestant invention though retained longest by them. It was the practice of many a devout medieval Christian. Zwingli merely took it to the logical conclusion in only having the eucharist celebrated at those four occasions each year at which his congregation had been accustomed to commune: Christmas, Easter, Pentecost, and the local patronal festival in September. His reasoning is clear: no communion, no eucharist.

Other reformers met strong opposition when they tried to persuade the laity to break centuries-old habits. That Luther met with more success than is usually assumed is seen by the fact that as late as Bach's time, thousands of Lutherans in Leipzig and Dresden received communion each Sunday. If there were many communicants the service could last three or four hours.[27] Calvin had less success; the magistrates in Geneva were obdurate. He would have had a weekly eucharist but in this instance did not get his way so Calvin recorded his chagrin. He attributes the practice of yearly communion to "a veritable invention of the devil" and says it should be received "at least once a week."[28] Most Anabaptists followed Zwingli in deeming four celebrations a year about right.

The Church of England, by demanding that there be no private masses but always "four, or three at the least [to] communicate with the priest," effectively did in frequent communion and three times a year became the minimum that the Canons of 1604 enumerated. Ironically, some of the small groups of English Separatists managed a weekly eucharist but the American Pilgrims had to forego this for nine years until an ordained minister emigrated to America to minister to them. Many Puritans took seriously the injunction of the *Westminster Directory* of 1645 that "the Communion, or Supper of the Lord is frequently to be celebrated" and this often meant monthly.[29] One important rule operated for Calvinists of all varieties; only the godly were allowed to come to the Lord's table. The fencing of tables ensured that only the truly penitent dared approach the table. Calvin is direct heir to the Fourth Lateran Council's decree in 1215 that penance was necessary to communion; he just enforced it more rigorously.

Anyone participating in Protestant eucharists would have noticed considerable reduction in ceremonial and general simplification of the service. Hubmaier's baptizing with a milk pail was matched by Zwingli celebrating the eucharist using the common wooden platters and cups that each housewife must have scrubbed (we hope) daily. The vessels must have spoken much louder than words.

The Puritans objected to many of the ceremonies retained in the *Book of Common Prayer*, ostensibly because they were without scriptural warrant. But one suspects that much ceremonial had simply become redundant when everything was done with words. We still speak of baptism as a cleansing flood so we do not bother to wash anyone.

A liturgical battle ensued in Russia during the seventeenth century. Patriarch Nikon, inspired by modern scholarship, attempted to renew the Orthodox liturgy on the basis of contemporary Greek texts. Ironically, the Russian texts he sought to repristinate were older than those then in use by the Greeks. He won the battle but alienated thousands of Old Believers.[30]

What did all these changes mean for the generations who lived through them? For Roman Catholics, the changes might have seemed unnoticeable in the sixteenth century but major shifts in piety awaited them in the seventeenth. Trent was determined to safeguard the old ways of understanding what the church experienced in the eucharist. So the presence of Christ was not only affirmed but Trent asserted that the conversion of the elements was most "aptly" (*aptissime*) called "transubstantiation," even though the meaning of the term may have shifted considerably since the Fourth Lateran Council used it in 1215.[31] The adoration of Christ in the eucharist was maintained and processions of the consecrated elements "through the streets and public places" defended.

Luther's doctrine seemed very similar although he vehemently repudiated the term transubstantiation. His people must have been hard put to find much difference between the old doctrine and his affirmation that Christ was present in, with, and under the bread and wine on a thousand altars. But there was no mistaking the differences between Luther and Zwingli. Both sides failed to agree at the Marburg Colloquy in 1529 for, as Luther remarked, "Our spirit is different from yours" even though they could agree on fourteen other articles out of the fifteen.

Zwingli had little concern about the physical elements, for Christ's human nature was in heaven and not on the altar. But Christ's divine nature transformed the congregation by uniting it in recollection of Christ. Thus the communion fellowship of the people, so long neglected in medieval piety, was elevated to the forefront of interest. Christ was present in the eucharist. Christ's actions were by a divine and spiritual nature, a transubstantiating, in effect, of the hearts of the people rather than the communion elements. Zwingli was not a child of the Enlightenment but resident in a still sacral universe where God did act. By and large, Anabaptist thought was similar.

Calvin, on the other hand, had a much higher value for signs. Because of our depravity, we need outward signs and God, who as our Creator knows us best, provides them in the sacraments: God "imparts spiritual things under visible ones." In the eucharist, through the vehicle of the Holy Spirit, we are led to heaven where we feed on Christ. The means is a mystery: "What, then, our mind does not comprehend, let faith conceive: that the Spirit truly unites things separated in space."[32]

Cranmer, however, favored Zwingli, though he placed a higher value on the sacrament and wanted more frequent celebrations. The Scots at least initially favored Calvin and insisted that the elements were far more than "naked and bare signs." Ironically, the Puritans seemed content with the Cranmerian theology of presence. It remained for the Quakers completely to spiritualize it so that communion was purely inward and all outward signs only a distraction from God.

One other theological issue must have puzzled many of the faithful. That is the ways in which the eucharist represented a sacrifice. Some sources indicate that crude popular notions prevailed that the mass was simply a repetition of what Christ did on Calvary. Others argue that a more sophisticated view prevailed, that the faithful saw it as a representation of Calvary.[33] Even Trent condemned extortionary demands for stipends for saying masses but it did insist that "this sacrifice is truly propitiatory." Luther railed against a system that had tended to treat the mass as merchandise to be peddled for a price. It conflicted, of course, with his whole case against works righteousness.

Other Protestant reformers took generally similar positions. Luther's solution in the mass was to discard the entire canon, "that mangled and abominable thing gathered from much filth and scum," except for the words of institution. In a sense, this brought the whole medieval emphasis on those words alone as effecting consecration to a logical conclusion; all else was unnecessary. Cranmer's solution was more ingenious; in 1552 he cut the canon in two and placed the sacrificial portions after all the elements had been consumed. He also could accept a few sacrificial concepts as biblical: the mass as a memorial of Christ, as a sacrifice of praise and thanksgiving (Heb. 13:15), and as a sacrifice of ourselves (Rom. 12:1). But it remained to Wesley in the eighteenth century to speak in positive terms of the eucharist as it implies a sacrifice.

What, then, did the people bring to the eucharist? Much survived of the medieval penitential piety, and Cranmer's phrase

"We be not worthy so much as to gather up the crumbs under thy table" is the most memorable image of this whole period and a neat summation of both medieval tendencies and Reformation biblicalism (Matt. 15:27). This fear of unworthiness certainly persisted. Ironically, it crops up in seventeenth-century Jansenism, a rather Calvinistic form of Catholicism in the low countries and France. Frequent communion was resisted on the grounds of human unworthiness.

For Protestants, the absence of penance tended to overload the eucharist, forcing it to do the work of two sacraments, forgive sins and receive Christ. For Calvin's followers, the fencing of the tables made the eucharist a means of disciplining the community. In Scotland, this came to take the form of sacramental seasons in which the whole community spent several days preparing for rare celebrations of the eucharist. One might attend such seasons in neighboring parishes at different times.[34] The moralistic approach to the eucharist is inescapable in the Reformed and Puritan traditions and even today is reflected by insisting on a general confession at the beginning of every eucharist.

Catholic eucharistic piety developed in a new direction in the seventeenth century. Jungmann says that "the Baroque spirit and . . . the traditional liturgy . . . were two vastly different worlds."[35] In essence, the eucharist came to be treated as the relic par excellence and the cult of the sacrament replaced the medieval fascination with relics, now left for tourists to gape at rather than for pilgrims to adore. Altar-tables became thrones for monstrances, appurtenances in which the consecrated host was displayed. Exposition (viewing the host) became a popular devotion and the service of Benediction focused on seeing (but not consuming) the host. The tabernacle (holding the consecrated bread) came to dominate the altar-table. All this came amid magnificent triumphalist architecture. The visual had come to an even greater ascendancy but it meant a complete revisioning of what church space was meant to be. Even though the text of the Roman mass was fixed from 1570 until 1970, eucharistic piety was by no means static but continued to evolve.

For Protestants, the chief positive gain was the new communal sense of the eucharist. Zwingli's often maligned approach had the merit that it focused on corporate experience of the very real work of Christ. The sense of being made one with Christ and one with each other is central for him and most other Protestant reformers. It was a step away from the individualistic obsession with one's own salvation that often plagued late medieval eucharistic piety. Regaining the ancient concept of communion fellowship was an important advance.

Christian Time

A wide variety of possibilities emerged with regard to the observance of time. For Roman Catholics, this involved basically a pruning of the saints' days which obstructed the systematic recital of the psalter in the daily office. No major new feast days had been added to the calendar since Corpus Christi in the fourteenth century. But the seeds of what was to be the Feast of the Sacred Heart began to sprout in this period although the feast was not authorized until 1765 and raised to first rank in 1856. With its themes of reparation for offenses to divine love in the eucharist, it was promoted by John Eudes and the visions of Margaret Mary Alacoque, both of seventeenth-century France. The other changes basically involved which saints were in or out of the calendar.

Luther's reforms endeavored to keep the major festivals of the historic year with the long established epistle and gospel lessons. His chief reform was "to observe only the Lord's days and the festivals of the Lord. We think that all the feasts of the saints should be abrogated, or if anything in them deserves it, it should be brought into the Sunday sermon."[36] He retained Circumcision, Epiphany, Purification, and Annunciation as dominical feasts but had a particular distaste for feasts of the Holy Cross.

Luther's reservations were mild compared to the Reformed, Anabaptist, and Puritan traditions. Here the Anglican tradition was the most conservative. Propers for the eucharist were provided for a number of New Testament saints and All Saints' Day. These saints' days commemorated apostles and evangelists, John the Baptist, Michel and All Angels, Stephen, Innocents, and Mary Magdalene. The introits for these (and all Sundays) were dropped in 1552.

Such things the Scots treated with impatience, denying that these human inventions should be tolerated "because in God's Scriptures they neither have commandments nor assurance, we judge utterly to be abolished from this realm."[37] But Scots and Puritans more than made up in strict observance of the Lord's Day as the Christian sabbath. This was to be kept with "a holy cessation, or resting all the day, from all unnecessary labors; and an abstaining not only from all sports and pastimes, but also from all worldly words and thoughts."[38] Other than public worship, the day was to be devoted to "reading, meditation, repetition of sermons, . . . holy conferences, prayer, . . . psalms, visiting the sick, relieving the poor, and such like duties of piety, charity and mercy, accounting the Sabbath a delight."[39]

One major change they did sanction and that was the provision "upon special emergent occasions, to separate a day or days for public fasting or thanksgiving, as the several eminent and extraordinary dispensations of God's providence shall administer cause and opportunity to his people."[40] God's past actions were not to be commemorated by special days; God's present actions were to be very much heeded. The Separatists at Plymouth, whom we know as the Pilgrims, kept just such a day in 1621 and we still observe it as Thanksgiving Day. Of course when crops were bad, or some of their shipping was sunk, or the Native Americans were troublesome, fasting days were the appropriate response to God's actions. This sense of the immediacy of God's actions in history certainly evokes a world before the Enlightenment.

Quakers refused to acknowledge any holy days, even taking offense at the naming of days and months after pagan gods. The solution was to speak of the first day or second month.

Pastoral Rites

Even greater variety appeared with the observance of the various pastoral rites. Extreme unction soon disappeared in Protestant circles but the natural rites of passage, marriage and burial, survived although secularized in some cases.

1. Reconciliation. For Roman Catholics, very little changed with regard to penance. The medieval verities were maintained: "confession should be complied with, at least once a year, by all and each,"[41] preferably in Lent, and only to a priest or bishop. It was asserted that this was the original practice. The chief innovation was the growing practice of erecting confessional booths in churches so priests would not have to be unprotected from women since confession was necessarily in private. Charles Borremeo (1538–1584), Cardinal Archbishop of Milan, was one of the promoters of this innovation which lasted until the 1970s.

Martin Luther had a very high opinion of penance although he reluctantly admitted it did not meet his definition of a sacrament.[42] He provided two forms for confession to a priest (1529 and 1531) although he was willing to assert that any Christian, by virtue of baptism, could pronounce another forgiven. He deplored the confession of sins by numbers and types but advocated confession of all that burdened one's conscience. Nor were satisfactions to be imposed to receive God's absolution.

Zwingli declericalizes it even further, insisting that James 5:16 ("Confess your sins one to another") means simply that one "makes sufficient confession who trusts in God," "who praises Him, . . . who acknowledges his sins and deplores them before the Lord, as . . . who fervently prays for forgiveness with the help of brethren."[43] There is "no need of any priest" consequently "let us, therefore, confess frequently to the Lord."

Reformed eucharistic liturgies took most seriously the prayer of confession at the beginning of the mass. Martin Bucer added the Decalogue as a means of public examination of conscience and this until recently was part of the eucharist in Reformed, Anglican, and Methodist rites. Calvin judges the ancient observance of penance "holy and wholesome" but modern practice is "less necessary, . . . a thing indifferent," a rather mild negative for him but baptism is the true "sacrament of penance." His eucharistic rite sees to it that all worshipers thoroughly purge themselves of sin by public confession.

Among the Anabaptists, discipline was strongly enforced by placing the ban on all serious transgressors and shunning them. But the purpose always was healing and the penitent sinner would be welcomed back into the community with the laying on of hands. Tertullian would have recognized the process if not the details of it.

A penitential order was grafted onto morning prayer in the Anglican tradition in 1552, reshaping it into an introspective rite rather than just prayer and praise. At the same time, the addition of the Decalogue to the opening moments of the eucharist heightened its penitential cast. The *Westminster Directory* provided a long list of intriguing forms of sins to move the "hearers hearts to be rightly affected with their sins" as part of the prayer before the sermon or "long prayer." Penance had not disappeared but simply been made corporate and public.

2. *Healing*. Rites of healing hardly recovered from their medieval association with rites of dying, at least for western Christians. Trent insists that extreme unction had been instituted by Christ and "insinuated" by Mark but calls it "the sacrament of the departing," hardly what Mark 16 means. The Council claims that James 5 refers to priests when it mentions the "elders." Luther has little patience with extreme unction as practiced in his day but he does favor prayer for the sick and argues that "elders" simply refers to "older, graver, and saintly men." Calvin is more blunt in criticism of existing practice: "these fellows smear with their grease not the sick but half-dead corpses when they are already drawing their last breath."[44] He recognizes the value of prayer for the sick and is aware that in Augustine's time all Christians could anoint the sick.

In the Church of England, a rite for visitation of the sick is provided. It exhorts the sick person to accept sickness with patience as "the chastisement of the Lord." There is also "The Communion of the Sick" which in 1549 may be from elements reserved from a celebration in the parish church earlier that day but in 1552 must be a new celebration in the sick room.

Unfortunately, the lack of an existing model of healing the sick led to the absence of any real efforts at services directed toward healing. Anointing disappeared entirely from Protestantism, not to be revived until the pietist Church of the Brethren in the eighteenth century.

3. *Christian Marriage*. Marriage rites were a social necessity but a variety of practices ensued. Trent tried to regularize practices in the decree *Tametsi* but with uncharacteristic openness decreed "if any provinces have in this matter other laudable customs and

ceremonies in addition to the aforesaid, the holy council wishes earnestly that they be by all means retained."[45] The Council, composed entirely of celibates, claimed that it was "better and more blessed to remain in virginity, or in celibacy, than to be united in matrimony." The *Roman Ritual* of 1614 contained the official marriage rite but many local customs persevered.

Marriage rites tend to be conservative since so much is at stake. Protestants all agreed (except for Count Nicholas Von Zinzendorf in the eighteenth century) that marriage was not a sacrament. On the other hand, as Luther said "it should be accounted a hundred times more spiritual than the monastic estate." His marriage rite of 1529 follows local custom in a simple exchange of vows and rings at the church entrance, Matthew 19:6 "What God has joined . . .," and pronouncement of marriage before entering the church to hear the second creation account Genesis 2:18, 21-24 and other passages read, a blessing, and most likely a sermon.

Calvin's marriage rite occurs in the Sunday service before the sermon. It is a public service totally inside the building. Later, the *Westminster Directory* advised that weddings not be on the Lord's Day or days of humiliation. The Puritans discarded the ring ceremony.

By the time of the 1549 Anglican prayerbook, the service was entirely inside. It follows the late medieval Sarum rite although without the bride's promise "to be bonere and boxsum in bedde and attebord." The ends of marriage are still the medieval priorities: procreation, remedy against sin, and mutual society. It was the Puritans who reversed those priorities. Converts to Anabaptist groups might be retrothed although previously married, just as priests might be reordained if elected to pastor a congregation. Quaker couples simply spoke their vows to each other in meetings, ironically affirming all that western sacramental theology required.

4. Christian Burial. Burial patterns shifted. Luther wanted to abolish "the popish abominations, such as vigils, masses for the dead, processions, purgatory, and all other hocus-pocus on behalf of the dead." He wanted funerals to proclaim the resurrection with "comforting hymns." Anything that suggested purgatory was to be avoided. In a certain sense, we can speak of the secularization of burial. The Reformed and Puritan traditions are firm: the body is to be accompanied to the grave and buried without any ceremony. Afterwards the minister may go to the church and preach on death and resurrection.

The Anglican order is a bit fuller, consisting of the committal, reading of I Corinthians 15, and a few prayers. The *Roman Ritual* of 1614 is much more extensive, including stations at the home, the church, and the grave. A large portion of it is psalmody. Essentially it incorporates Roman practice of the time. It provides for a funeral mass and final rite of absolution. There is a separate rite for the burial of children which presumes an age of innocence if they die baptized before the age of reason.

LIVING TOGETHER IN COMMUNITY

Leadership

Roman Catholics were firmly committed to keeping leadership roles intact with no change. Although ordination was not discussed in Trent until very late (July 1563), the Council asserted that ordination was a sacrament and that those "marked with the clerical tonsure should ascend through the lesser to the greater orders"[46] and condemned the notion "that all Christians indiscriminately are priests of the New Testament." The ordination rites were standardized under Pope Clement VIII in the *Roman Pontifical* of 1596. They followed very closely the late medieval rites of Durandus. Innovation was not the order of the day.

Not much less conservative were the churches of Sweden and Finland. Although Lutheran, they did not share Luther's rather pragmatic views on ordination (he ordained a bishop although a priest himself). The apostolic succession was resolutely kept in Sweden and recovered in the nineteenth century in Finland after a lapse.

At least outwardly, the Church of England was equally conservative, retaining the orders of bishop, priest, and deacon, although abolishing minor orders and tonsure. Cranmer's first ordinal appeared in 1550 and was revised in 1552. Much of it is dependent upon Martin Bucer, the Strasbourg reformer who had emigrated to England in 1549. Paul Bradshaw believes "the reason for Cranmer's close dependence on Bucer and almost total rejection of the wording of the medieval rites, in contrast to his usual use of sources in compiling the Prayer Book, is almost certainly to be found in his denial of the popular view of the sacrifice of the Mass and of the sacrificial priesthood."[47] Cranmer apparently did not think of the episcopate as a distinct order but as a function, although the rite can accommodate the former interpretation. He emphasized the litany and imposition of hands and realized that the tradition of instruments was subsidiary ceremonial.

By contrast, the early Luther is quite radical, insisting that ministry is purely functional. Here is true liturgical equality "for whoever comes out of the water of baptism can boast that he is already a consecrated priest, bishop and pope, although of course it is not seemly that just anybody should exercise such office. . . . There is no true, basic difference between laymen and priests, . . . except for the sake of office and work, but not for the sake of status."[48] Later on, Luther was more inclined to stress ordained ministry as a gift of Christ to the Church. He produced a rite for "The Ordination of Ministers of the Word" in 1539 which is quite radical, culminating in the presbyters imposing their hands on the ordinands while the principal ordinator says the Lord's Prayer.[49]

Zwingli considered ordination "a human invention" but Calvin has a high view of "the true office of presbyter" and hints that he would have considered presbyteral ordination a sacrament except that "it is not ordinary or common with all believers."[50] Uncharacteristically, he gives up the clearly biblical use of laying on of hands at ordination. He rails against the sevenfold orders and the notion of a sacrificial priesthood and instead proposes pastors, teachers, elders, and deacons as "four orders of office instituted by our Lord for the government of his Church."[51]

Although Calvin ends up with a tightly organized government in which rule is by professional clergy and lay rulers, all set aside by ordination, the Anabaptists developed a much freer form in which local congregations chose one of their members for leadership, ordained him (or sometimes reordained if already a priest), and frequently had to replace him soon after martyrdom.

For the Puritans, ministry is seen largely as ministry of the word although there were episcopal, presbyteral, and congregational Puritans. The basis of the minister's authority is as scholar of God's word. The *Westminster Directory* is silent about ordination but very explicit on the skills requisite for preaching: painfully, plainly, faithfully, wisely, gravely, "with loving affection," and "as taught of God." Among American Puritans, ordination followed call by a congregation after the gathering of a new congregation. If other ministers were not available, the laity performed the laying on of hands, so-called "plebeian ordination." This gradually gave way to what Horton Davies calls a "clericalization of ordination" as ministers of neighboring churches were invited to lay on hands.[52]

These problems never arose for Quakers since all were treated as equal. Traveling Friends (or itinerant preachers) might be recognized, as were "recorded ministers" (those who spoke frequently in meetings), but these were purely functional distinctions and not of status. Women could and did fulfill all roles including being among the first of the North American martyrs (Boston, 1660). Quakers were among the first Protestant missionaries. The Society of Friends first achieved what Christianity had never known before, true liturgical democracy. Their contribution to combining worship and justice is unequaled and still stands as a challenge to other churches. George Fox (1624–1691), the founder of the Society of Friends, remains the greatest figure in the relatively short history of liturgy and justice.

Preaching

For all concerned, the Reformation era represented a reawakening of the importance of preaching. In this instance, conservatism is hard to measure. Roman Catholicism saw a great increase in preaching, especially after Trent mandated sermons on all Sundays and holy days although this was not fulfilled in many churches. Controversial sermons flourished in areas of religious conflict. The Jesuits, particularly, distinguished themselves in preaching campaigns. Their churches were designed specifically with the acoustical needs of preaching in mind and the pulpit became an important liturgical center.

In seventeenth-century France, there was a period of brilliant pulpit rhetoric, led by Jacques Bossuet, a distinguished court preacher. Others, particularly Jean-Baptiste Massillon and François de Fenelon carried on this tradition. Their sermons seemed largely to reflect the sophisticated ears of their audiences, full of classical devices of rhetoric, but not as genuine liturgical preaching as part of the mass.

Luther is often referred to as the father of Protestant preaching. He certainly made it a central part of ministry and worship, claiming that preaching should occur whenever Christians gathered for any form of worship. There were three sermons on Sunday in Wittenberg and daily throughout the week. Most were based on biblical texts. Suddenly confronted with the task of teaching many former priests to preach, Luther produced a series of postils or sermon collections to be imitated.

Luther's sermons are basically scriptural, usually affirming a literal interpretation rather than allegorical. It is an intrinsic part of both the mass and daily office for him. Brilioth argues that "to the extent Luther oriented his preaching liturgically, the liturgy continued to be a living resource for Lutheran Christendom."[53]

After Luther, what more can one say? Even the Quakers found "threshing meetings" or outdoors preaching to reach converts to be a vital form of witness, although their own meetings were without sermons. No one could surpass Luther in his commitment to sound biblical preaching. Zwingli surrendered the classical biblical pericopes in favor of preaching his way in course through entire books of scripture. This became the preferred Reformed pattern and contributed to the setting aside of the traditional Christian year. The prophesying in Zurich gave the congregation an opportunity to respond to the preacher's handling of a text. Such a practice survived clandestinely among Puritan preachers in the Church of England during Queen Elizabeth's reign and burst into open practice in Puritan America. This gave the congregation the last word but the practice disappeared in the revivals of the eighteenth-century Great Awakening. Calvin preached Sundays on New Testament books and weekdays from the books of the Old Testament. Two thousand of his sermons survive. Exegesis is foremost but careful application to daily life is never absent. Brilioth considers "the exegetical and the prophetic" to be the "two basic characteristics in the Calvinistic tradition of preaching."[54]

Anglicans, too, saw the importance of liturgical preaching. Cranmer imitated Luther by publishing model sermons in 1547 in the *Book of Homilies* and the bishops added another in 1563. Puritans tended to spurn those "dumb dogs" of preachers who relied on such packaged sermons and insisted on preachers who carefully did their own exegesis and prepared their own sermons. Anglicanism had its own share of distinguished preachers from the days of the martyred bishops Hooper, Ridley, and Latimer, to such eloquent seventeenth-century preachers as Lancelot Andrewes, John Donne, and Jeremy Taylor.

Church Music

If the Reformation period saw an explosion in preaching, it was no less dramatic in the increase in music, particularly as regards congregational singing. This was far from universal and Roman Catholic and Zwinglian congregations remained largely mute while Lutherans and Anabaptists burst into song. So who are the real conservatives here? Many of the problems revolved around the availability of musical talent and imagination.

For those Roman Catholic parishes and religious communities with an abundance of talent, the mass became an imposing concert of performance music. Ever since the ninth century, an alternative to the chant had been developing in the form of polyphonic music with different words and melodies sung simultaneously. By the end of the twelfth century, composers were writing for three or four voices and polyphony had become a distinct alternative to plainsong. This demanded competent musicians, not ordinary lay folk. The Renaissance era saw many great composers of motets and full masses in polyphony: Lassus, Palestrina, Gabrieli, Victoria, Monteverdi, and Byrd. Notable, too, was the development of the pipe organ to accompany singing and to play purely instrumental music. Late medieval cathedrals and large churches had great pipe organs.

Luther exulted in music, regarding it as one of God's greatest gifts. He endeavored to structure the *German Mass* so major portions of it could be sung in German paraphrase. Even the lessons are chanted by the priest and the congregation joins in singing such ordinary parts as the Creed ("In One True God We All Believe") and the German *Sanctus* which is a paraphrase of Isaiah 6. By the end of 1523, while the mass was still in Latin, Luther had begun to write vernacular hymns and the next year he supervised the publication of *Spiritual Hymn Booklet* with the help of his musical assistant, Johann Walter. Since poets also wrote their own music at this time, Luther was also a composer. Altogether, he is credited with about 37 hymns. By the end of the sixteenth century, a whole series of hymns of the day had been codified to accompany each gospel reading in the Lutheran Sunday service. The congregation participated fully and vigorously in the singing of hymns as well as the rest of the liturgy. Lutheran liturgy and musical liturgy had become synonymous.

The contrast with Zwingli could not have been greater. The best musician of the Reformers, Zwingli had composed motets and was a master of many instruments. His forbidding of any music began with the elimination of singing in 1523 and destruction of the pipe organs in 1527. It is likely that his reasons were that scripture must be followed at all costs[55] although there are some hints that, had he lived longer, he might have found a place for some song.[56]

Calvin, again, provided a compromise position. Music was welcome as long as the words were scriptural. This meant the singing of psalms which was made possible by turning them into metrical paraphrases. Calvin hired good musicians such as Claude Goudimel and Louis Bourgeois, while a poet, Clement Marot, provided French texts. Calvin's service book is entitled *The Form of Prayers and Ecclesiastical Songs* (1542). Visitors to Geneva were impressed by the fervor and joy of the singing of psalms.

Anabaptists went beyond their mentor, Zwingli, and burst into hymnody without the Calvinist inhibitions about scriptural texts. Early on they began to publish hymnals; the *Ausbund* of 1560 is still in use among the Old Order Amish. A distinctive hymnody developed which reflected the persecutions they endured, a rich hymody of martyrdom. Even today, groups such as the Mennonites sing hymns without accompaniment.

The Calvinist solution became the *de facto* position of the Church of England. Cranmer was not opposed to hymnody but lamented the lack of poets to produce hymns in English. His own translation of the *Veni Creator Spiritus* proved that his gifts in prose did not extend to poetry. So metrical paraphrases of psalms became the staple of Anglican congregational song until the mid-nineteenth century. The Old Version by Thomas Sternhold and John Hopkins eventually yielded to the *New Version of the Psalms* (1696) by Nahum Tate and Nicholas Brady. A rich tradition of choral music in cathedrals and collegiate churches was recognized in the 1662 *Book of Common Prayer* with provision for an anthem at morning and evening prayer.

Faithful to Calvin, the Puritans restricted singing to the psalms, usually in metrical versions. This began to change, despite stubborn opposition, when Isaac Watts commenced writing hymns at the end of the seventeenth century, moving from making David "sing like a Christian" ("Our God, Our Help in Ages Past") to explicitly Christian hymns ("When I Survey the Wondrous Cross").

Church Architecture

Once again, church architecture sums up the changes of this period. Most traditions except Anabaptists and Quakers inherited large numbers of medieval buildings as state churches. Massive programs of new church building did not get underway until the seventeenth century and then only as a result of fires, wars, colonization, and missionary activities. But every group had much to do with the reordering of existing buildings as well as occasional iconoclasm.[57]

It is not easy to say which tradition was the most conservative. Many items of liturgical art survived in Lutheran lands that might have been destroyed in Roman Catholic areas and certainly were in Reformed and Anglican contexts.

Roman Catholics destroyed much medieval art as archaic and barbaric in the eyes of Renaissance people. Some medieval images, such as God the Father with a long beard, were no longer acceptable. But more important, the concept of space underwent a drastic change in the baroque era. The paradigmatic building was the main Jesuit church in Rome, Il Gesu, built 1550–1572. Not only did the choir disappear as a distinct space, not only was preaching accommodated by careful consideration of acoustics, but the whole space became a theatrical setting for the mass. In these new churches, roodscreens disappear and the chancel is more a stage, as in the theater. Stage design influenced the churches the Jesuits built in Rome and soon all over the world.[58] A highly centralized architectural agency reproduced the new type of church space with great efficiency. It was a revolution in church building.

Lutheran church building began with the Castle Chapel at Torgau in 1544. Dominant themes emerged in stressing both visibility and audibility. Much of the baroque appealed to Lutheran tastes, especially a bright burst of light over the altar-table. A form that gradually became common was altar-table, pulpit, and font gathered together in one place at the front of the church.

For the Reformed tradition, everything tended to focus on the centrality of the pulpit. Balconies became an earmark of Reformed churches since they brought many people within hearing distance of the preacher. For the eucharist, tables were placed across the front or down the aisles and the congregation sat around them at communion. The fonts were usually modest basins attached to the pulpit. The form of the building could vary but they were mostly central, i.e., square, Greek cross, or circular, with the pulpit in the most prominent location.

Anabaptists had to be content with modest structures, focusing chiefly on an extended pulpit that might accommodate several preachers. For Quakers, the whole building was congregational space except for aisles. The entire focus was on the community, gathered for worship, and not on any liturgical center, even a pulpit.

A series of changes marked Anglican architecture during this period. Under Edward VI, there was a great deal of iconoclasm with the intent of removing anything idolatrous from churches. Nearly a century later, the Puritans completed the process in parts of England. The most noticeable change was the adaptation of medieval churches for Protestant worship. The chancels were turned into eucharistic rooms for communicants. In the sixteenth century, many altars were demolished in favor of tables set lengthwise in the chancel. "It had been generally accepted firstly that churches should in effect be two separate rooms with the chancel for the sacrament and the nave for preaching, and secondly that in the nave pulpit and reading-desk should be placed at the east end."[59] In the 1630s many altar-tables were replaced against the east wall, enclosed by a new item, communion rails. After the great London fire of 1666, Sir Christopher Wren brought new sophistication to a one room church space, built on "auditory" principles for best hearing the service read and preaching.

America provided a vast laboratory for experiments in church building for both Anglicans and Puritans. They have in common that they are single-space structures. Anglican churches have a prominent altar-table although the chief focus was on the center for reading the service, often a triple-decker (clerk's desk, reading desk, and pulpit). Puritan meeting houses are dominated by elegant pulpits, often in front of a round-headed pulpit window. A table top might be hinged to the pew in front of the pulpit for use on eucharistic Sundays. All in all, this was an exciting period in church architecture as all traditions scrambled to find new architectural forms to express the worship developments they were experiencing.

FOR FURTHER READING

Blume, Friedrich, et al. *Protestant Church Music*. London: Victor Gollancz, 1975.

Cuming, G. J. *A History of Anglican Liturgy*. Second edition. London: Macmillan, 1982.

Cuming, G. J., and R. C. D. Jasper. *Prayers of the Eucharist: Early and Reformed*. Third edition. New York: Pueblo Publishing Company, 1987.

Davies, Horton. *The Worship of the American Puritans, 1629–1730.* New York: Peter Lang, 1990.

————. *The Worship of the English Puritans.* Westminster: Dacre Press, 1948.

Hageman, Howard G. *Pulpit and Table.* Richmond: John Knox Press, 1962.

Old, Hughes Oliphant. *The Patristic Roots of Reformed Worship.* Zurich: Theologischer Verlag, 1975.

Reed, Luther D. *The Lutheran Liturgy.* Revised edition. Philadelphia: Fortress Press, 1960.

Rowell, Geoffrey. *The Liturgy of Christian Burial.* London: Alcuin Club/S.P.C.K., 1977.

Senn, Frank, ed. *Protestant Spiritual Traditions.* Mahwah, N.J.: Paulist Press, 1986.

Thompson, Bard. *Liturgies of the Western Church.* Cleveland: World Publishing Company, 1961.

Vajta, Vilmos. *Luther on Worship.* Philadelphia: Muhlenberg Press, 1958.

White, James F. *Protestant Worship: Traditions in Transition.* Louisville: Westminster/John Knox Press, 1989.

————. *Protestant Worship and Church Architecture.* New York: Oxford University Press, 1964.

CHAPTER V

Worship in the Churches of Modern Times

The past three centuries have been some of the most lively in the whole history of Christian worship with abundant positive contributions. In the eighteenth and nineteenth centuries, Protestant worship underwent sweeping changes. To make up for lost time, Roman Catholics made changes even more drastic in the twentieth century. The western churches have borrowed much from the East in modern times; the eastern churches have also westernized in many ways. In this period, we find patterns both centrifugal—an ever widening variety of possibilities in worship—and centripedal—a growing consensus on what is essential in worship.

The period from 1700 to the present begins with the impact of the Enlightenment on worship, a reorientation as great as that of the sixteenth-century Reformation. Liturgical scholars tend to avoid the Enlightenment; few find much reason to study the eighteenth century and even fewer find anything to praise in it.

Our center of liturgical interest also shifts westward from Europe to America. Although Europeans have had almost a monopoly on the writing of liturgical history, for a century and a half North Americans have been quietly (and sometimes not so quietly) changing the history of Christian worship. Thus we shall have to look homeward to discover these missing chapters in liturgical histories.

North America also provides the staging area for many liturgical developments initiated by missionaries in South America, Africa, and Asia. Future histories may have to concentrate on those areas in delineating the development of Christian worship in the next century.

This period is also marked by the maturing of liturgical scholarship and the impact of ecumenism. For the first time in history, liturgists have helped to shape the progress of Christian worship by drawing on findings of liturgical history, liturgical theology, and ritual studies. And what each scholar recovers has become available for all regardless of tradition. Borrowing from similar sources in the early church has led to many similar reforms.

THE WORLD OF MODERN TIMES

The first great fact of this period is the Enlightenment, *Aufklärung,* or Age of Reason. It stands as a huge watershed from which everything drains in a different direction than in the Medieval and Reformation periods. The human mind underwent a paradigm shift in this period, very roughly coterminous with the eighteenth century. It has never recovered. Despite reactions in the nineteenth century against the excesses of Enlightenment rationalism, the whole modern period is predicated on the supremacy of human reason against any form of external authority.

As the Age of Reason, the Enlightenment challenged all forms of authority and elevated individual judgement to question everything previous ages simply accepted whether in politics, religion, science, or any other area. Previous ages never found it necessary to defend Christianity purely on the grounds of reasonableness; miracles had sufficed to give it credibility. The Enlightenment, while not necessarily godless, changed entirely the grounds on which religion could be defended.

The Great Seal of the United States speaks of the beginning of a new age in 1776. It was certainly that for the human mind in western civilization. An interesting reflection in the American landscape is that the east coast states are laid out in a familiar European pattern following the contours of the land; the western two thirds are laid out in a strictly mathematical grid of one mile intervals. Something had happened to our perception of space as in so many other forms of being.

The changes in worship could not escape such a shift in human consciousness but various traditions reacted differently. In his *Religion within the Limits of Reason Alone,* published in 1793, Immanuel Kant spoke of "three kinds of *illusory faith* . . . the faith in *miracles,* . . . the faith in *mysteries* . . . the faith in *means of grace.*"[1] He discusses the sacraments of baptism and holy communion in which he finds some merit so long as they are not seen as "*a means of grace*—this is a religious illusion which can do naught but work counter to the spirit of religion."[2] The traditional view that God uses the sacraments as means of grace is anathema for Kant. The essence of religion seems to be the pursuit of virtue. Worship is all right so long as it produces virtue.

It is easy to see what a challenge this was to the traditional view, shared by Catholics and Protestants alike, that God acted in worship in gracious self giving. The Enlightenment believed in God but it was a God who had retired, leaving the world to run according to God's design. But it was not a God who intervened in self-giving love. God's past work in Jesus Christ was to be remembered, not experienced afresh.

Sacramental religion survived by several methods. The first was simply to abide by the old interpretations and resolutely ignore any changes in the human mind. This led to a rather schizoid mentality but was basically the method chosen by Roman Catholicism up until the 1960s. The second was to appeal beyond reason to personal experience of God's gracious acts conveyed in the sacraments. This was the practice of early Methodism but it was difficult to transmit across the Atlantic or to succeeding generations.

The third possibility, and by far the most widespread in American Protestantism even today, is a biblicism that limits God's acts to our commemoration of them. Thus the human becomes not so much the recipient of sacraments but their performer. Sacraments become a way we remember what God did in times past. We do not experience them as present encounter with the Holy One. The Enlightenment did not rule out biblicism; rather it encouraged biblicism when it kept God out of the way as far as the present is concerned. So we find a situation today in which the sacraments are basically memorials to God's past actions in Jesus Christ. The sacraments endure because the Bible commands: "Go therefore and make disciples of all nations, baptizing them" and "do this in remembrance of me." An Enlightenment mentality governed the development of much of American Christianity even in, maybe especially in, those groups that often seem least enlightened. There is no way of understanding the dominant approach to the sacraments of most American Protestants (and not a few Roman Catholics) except in terms of Enlightenment concepts of a God who once acted but whose actions are now only known in memory.

The nineteenth century brought many reactions to the Enlightenment, particularly in the form of a Romanticism that glorified the past, revelled in the picturesque, and exalted feeling. But here too, feeling focused on the individual, just as the Enlightenment had concentrated on autonomous reason. Romanticism led both to neo-medievalism and to revivalism. Both glorified the individual's perception of things, for the individual was now the center of reality.

In this period, we see the addition of three major worship traditions to western Christianity: the Methodist, the Frontier, and the Pentecostal. The *Methodist Tradition* was in many ways a counter-cultural movement to the Enlightenment. While the Enlightenment downplayed sacramental worship, Methodism's founder, John Wesley (1703–1791) insisted on frequent communion, i.e., weekly when possible. When feelings were discounted, Methodism stressed heart religion; where zeal was discouraged, Methodists were accused of enthusiasm. The introduction of hymn singing gave Methodism a warmth lacking in the staid worship of the state church to which Methodism acted as a third order. But much of the sacramental side of Methodism sank somewhere while crossing the Atlantic, and American Methodism accommodated itself readily to the Enlightenment.

The nineteenth century saw an important new tradition develop on the American frontier, one which was to become the most prevalent form of worship in the United States. The *Frontier Tradition* had its origins in efforts to reach the unchurched scattered over the area beyond the Appalachians. By 1830, a third of the American population occupied this area. The Frontier Tradition was the first purely American tradition. As Emerson remarked, Europe extended to the Appalachians; America began beyond. The camp meeting became the fountainhead, itself derived from the Scots' sacramental seasons. In modern times, this tradition reaches scores of millions in the form of television worship.

The beginning of the twentieth century saw the origins of yet another major worship tradition, the *Pentecostal Tradition*. It is the first post-Enlightenment tradition in that it has no inhibitions about experiencing the reality of God's presence in worship. Spirit-filled gifts animate every service. Sacraments may seem a bit tame since the evidence of God's present activity is already so overwhelming. From the very beginning, blacks and women played major leadership roles in developing this tradition. Amazingly, the Holy Spirit made itself manifest in mainline Protestant churches (1960 on) and Roman Catholic churches (1967 on) so one must now distinguish between the "classical Pentecostals" and the "neo-Pentecostals" or "charismatics" within other churches.

We also need to say a brief word about Roman Catholicism during this period in order to avoid repetition. Theodor Klauser speaks of the period from 1588 to 1963 as that of "rigid unification in the liturgy and rubricism."[3] The official texts and rubrics of worship were tightly nailed down in a most untraditional effort to insure absolute uniformity everywhere in the world. Indian converts in California were to hear and see the same forms of worship as kings at Versailles. Piety, architecture, music, and many other unregulated aspects of Roman Catholic worship nevertheless went on evolving almost without interruption.

A major shift began in 1833 with the revival of monasticism in France, Germany, and Belgium after being nearly extinguished by forces brought on by the Enlightenment. The result was what we may call the first liturgical movement, based largely on restoration of lost glories of worship such as Gregorian chant. After World War II, a second liturgical movement arose. This was based not in monasteries but in parishes and took much of its agenda from Protestant worship. The movement scarcely existed outside of countries or individuals in direct contact with the Protestant use of the vernacular, emphasis on preaching, and congregational song. Vatican II brought a revolution in worship in which many of the things condemned by the Council of Trent were made standard procedure for western Catholicism. Protestants, in turn, returned the compliment by borrowing much from the post-Vatican II Catholic reforms, most noticeably the three-year lectionary, contemporary English instead of Elizabethan, and a plurality of liturgical forms. The result is that many of the differences between mainline Protestants and Roman Catholics have been obliterated. This development has probably gone as far as it is likely to at present. Evangelicals have been little affected in their worship life by these changes.

BECOMING CHRISTIAN

During this period, Christian initiation has been thoroughly discussed, resulting in much revision in practice and theology. The biggest issue has been the question of the proper candidates for baptism. Those who baptize infants (pedobaptists) have been opposed by those who insist on believer's baptism only (anti-pedobaptists). What is most strange is that some of the players have changed sides. The leading Reformed theologian of our century, Karl Barth,[4] delivered a strong attack on infant baptism and, more recently, some Roman Catholic theologians have questioned this practice. A major shift has come about in that those who practice believers' baptism only have become a mighty force, perhaps the largest group of Christians in America, if the Frontier and Pentecostal traditions be combined. Most of the groups that originated on the frontier and in the twentieth century have been anti-pedobaptist. Much of this is due in part to their Enlightenment background which made it impossible for them to think that God acted regardless of a conscious and active recipient. If sacraments depend upon human initiative, then certainly children are incapable of baptism. Problems have arisen for groups that have moved from being small sects, gathered from society, to church types, encompassing most members of society. This often leads to an increasing practice of the baptism of young, i.e., pre-school children who hardly fit the category of believers. Sect-type groups, such as the various Mennonite denominations, find that in a small tightly-disciplined community believers' baptism functions quite satisfactorily.

Problems arise in European countries where baptism of children, often without believing parents, especially in countries with state churches, has led to infant baptism being very much clouded. All Christians have deplored this practice but in 1980 the Roman Catholic Congregation for the Doctrine of Faith found it necessary to issue an *Instruction on Infant Baptism*,[5] defending its continuance. The debate over infant baptism continues although the arguments have not improved much, if at all, since the sixteenth century.

Some realignments have also occurred with regard to the mode of baptism. In his early years, John Wesley insisted on observing the rubrics of the *Book of Common Prayer*, although few of his contemporaries were willing to insist on dipping infants. Later in life, Wesley allowed pouring and sprinkling. Most of the groups originating on the frontier, and many of the Pentecostals, insist on immersion of adults as the only biblical mode. Ironically, by insisting on the fullness of the sacramental sign and that baptism always take place before the assembled church, they show a deeper sacramental instinct than many so-called sacramental churches that baptize infants in private with a minimum of water. Most Frontier Tradition churches refuse even to use the term "sacrament," preferring instead "ordinance," a rather legalistic reference to God's commands in scripture.

In recent decades in mainline Protestant and Roman Catholic churches, there has been an effort to recover baptism of all ages by immersion as a means of increasing the sign value of the sacrament. As yet, this is still only in a minority of parishes. In part, this failure is due to the lack of adequate fonts where immersion of adults and infants is possible. Meanwhile, over a

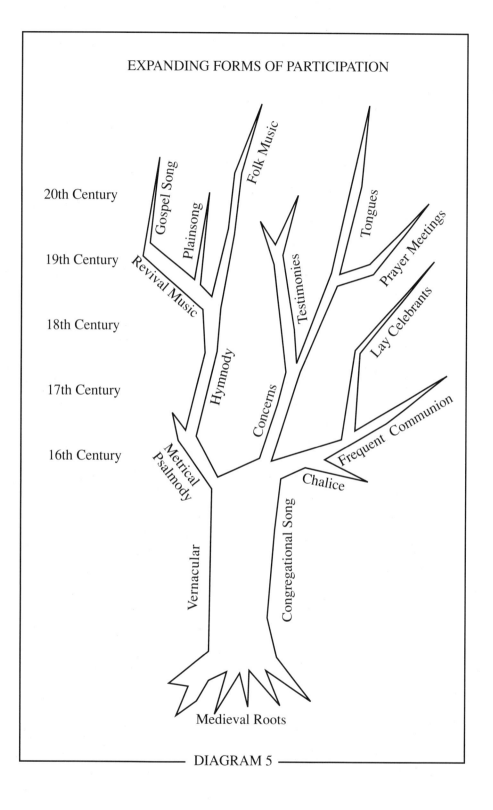

EXPANDING FORMS OF PARTICIPATION

20th Century

19th Century

18th Century

17th Century

16th Century

Gospel Song

Plainsong

Folk Music

Tongues

Prayer Meetings

Testimonies

Revival Music

Lay Celebrants

Hymnody

Concerns

Frequent Communion

Metrical Psalmody

Chalice

Vernacular

Congregational Song

Medieval Roots

DIAGRAM 5

hundred thousand churches in the United States, mostly evangelicals, have facilities designed for and practice the immersion of adult believers.

Another major shift has been the rearrangement of the separated parts of Christian initiation. A variety of factors has complicated the situation. John Wesley, while defending infant baptism, introduced a new factor, the importance of conversion. This did not acquire a symbolic act although it often did occur as a result of revivalistic preaching. Wesley eliminated the practice of confirmation. His American descendants, by mid-nineteenth century, added a probationary period for adult converts, symbolized by reception into church membership some six months after baptism. In the twentieth century, American Methodists changed this to preparatory membership for those baptized as infants who were then later received into church membership or (after 1964) confirmed.

The introduction of the category of conversion experience, new birth, or being born again came to have a major influence on much of the Frontier Tradition and evangelicals of every tradition. For many, it was a prerequisite for believers' baptism. For most, new birth was the real initiatory event of which subsequent baptism was simply a sign. Baptism signified what had already happened in the life of the individual and made it public.

One consequence of the new importance of conversion was to put into question the effects of baptism. Wesley defended the regeneration of infants at baptism, i.e., that baptism effected what it signified. Regeneration became increasingly problematic for evangelicals and others whose views of the sacraments were shaped by Enlightenment theories. The situation came to a head in the Church of England in 1847 when G. C. Gorham, an Anglican priest, refused to acknowledge that baptism effected regeneration instead of merely signifying it.[6] This has been a major problem between those who profess that God acts in baptism and those who see it as a human sign of profession.

The emphasis on the primacy of the conversion experience has lead to serious attempts to ritualize it. The most successful attempt has been the Rite of Christian Initiation of Adults (known as R.C.I.A.) which has come to play a major role in many Roman

Catholic parishes in America.[7] The R.C.I.A. recovers the process of the *Apostolic Tradition* of the third century. A congregation leads converts through a long process of stages of training, prayer, and examination of life until final initiation is reached in the sacraments of baptism, confirmation, and first communion. Confirmation is usually given by the parish priest.

Other western churches have been intrigued by the eastern churches' ability to keep alive the unity of all the rites of initiation at whatever age given. This has led to attempts within the Lutheran, Reformed, Anglican, and Methodist traditions to make initiation complete at whatever age, be it at birth or later in life. A new development is the renewal or reaffirmation of what God has done for us in baptism. This may be an annual congregational event in the yearly cycle, often at the Baptism of the Lord, Easter Vigil, Pentecost, or All Saints' Day. And renewal of baptism may be celebrated on occasion for lapsed individuals who have come home.

Baptism has become an item of increased concern in the twentieth century for a variety of reasons, not least of which has been ecumenism. It is the one sacrament for which no one questions the validity of other Christians' practice. It is also the sacrament in which equality among all persons is most apparent, hence it has been the source of crusades for justice within the churches. Initiation into the royal priesthood of Christ may be used as a basis for the ordination of women, as a plea for justice to all fellow members of the Body of Christ who are deprived, or as an assertion of the priestly vocation of all Christians. At the same time, baptism is sometimes seen as initiating us into a distinct life style, a sign that we at last are catching up with Luther's baptismal spirituality.

Although debates still flourish over the proper candidates, mode, and sequence of baptism, substantial agreement has been reached. The traditional baptismal formula has caused some new problems for those who consider the use of "Father" and "Son" to be masculine terms in this context. The 1982 document, *Baptism, Eucharist and Ministry* is a testimony to the level of agreement reached: "All agree that Christian baptism is in water and the Holy Spirit."[8] But it can also be read with a discerning eye as to the variety of contributions different churches have brought and also of the continuing existence of differing practices and belief. What distinguishes the twentieth century from previous ones is the effort made and considerable success achieved in seeing merits in a variety of practices and beliefs. Much is contingent; what works well for a Mennonite congregation does not necessarily imply that it should for a Roman Catholic parish. Recognition that diversity is an important part of church life is a most significant gain.

It is not too much to hope that the richness of the biblical metaphors for baptism are once again reasserting themselves. Thus baptism is not just one image but a variety of aspects of what it means to begin life anew in Jesus Christ.

LIVING AND DYING CHRISTIAN

Every aspect of the daily, weekly, yearly, and lifetime cycles of Christian worship has changed dramatically in the West in the last three centuries. Many of these changes reflect the social and intellectual currents of the Enlightenment; others mirror quite different influences.

Daily Public Prayer

Throughout much of this period, daily public prayer thrived in the Anglican Tradition where morning and evening prayer was said daily in English parish churches. The daily office also provided a major portion of the Sunday service in Anglican churches until it began to be replaced by a weekly eucharist in the light of the Catholic Revival in Anglicanism otherwise known as the Oxford Movement, Tractarianism, or Puseyism. This movement and its successors slowly restored the eucharist to the dominant position in Sunday worship. In England, the Shortened Services Act of 1872 was a sign of a switch in priorities although the transition is still in process. A major shift in the Victorian era was the introduction of vested choirs in parish churches to sing morning and evening prayers. This, plus the new technology of gas lighting, led to a new popularity for choral evensong.

152

The daily office fared less well in Lutheran circles. By 1790, it had been largely discontinued in German cities as the Enlightenment advanced into most areas. In some parts of Romania, Lutheran daily public prayer survived even into the twentieth century.[9] Current attempts to revive such forms of worship have not been particularly successful.

For Roman Catholics, daily public prayer remained during most of this period virtually the monopoly of clergy and those in religious orders. The breviary of 1568 was scarcely changed except for the occasional addition of new saints days. The monastic revival of the nineteenth century gave much attention to recovery of a sung office in choir, usually using the restored Gregorian chant.

Vatican II expressed the timid hope that "the laity, too, are encouraged to recite the divine office"[10] although it is buried in a chapter directed to the needs of clergy and religious. The reforms proposed sound similar to sixteenth-century Anglican accomplishments: morning and evening prayer "as the chief hours," psalms to be distributed over a longer period than a week (eventually four weeks), and more abundant scripture. The *Liturgy of the Hours*, when it was approved in 1971, retained Lauds, midday prayer, vespers, compline, and an office of readings for any time during the day. Despite numerous reforms, it still remains a monastic office and has had little success in parish life. Robert Taft says "the unwillingness to make a more radical break with not just the forms, but with the mentality of this [monastic tradition] past, has marred the recent reform of the Roman Office."[11] With its virtual indifference to the needs of ordinary people, the office represents the chief failure among the post-Vatican II liturgical books. The eucharist still remains the only real option for daily public worship for most lay people.

Various innovations developed during this period. Eighteenth-century Methodists began a weekly practice of classes to exercise spiritual direction, usually under the leadership of a lay person. These classes met together weekly as a company "seeking the power of godliness, united in order to pray together, to receive the word of exhortation, and to watch over one another in love, that they may help each other to work out their salvation."[12] Wesley's pragmatic traditionalism is also shown in his adapting the ancient vigil as the Watch Night service and the early agape as the love feast.

Out of these weekly meetings grew on American soil the midweek prayer meeting. This was truly popular religion, usually presided over by a lay person, and consisting of spontaneous prayer (in words and concerns highly repetitious), the singing of familiar hymns, and the reading of favorite scripture texts. In other words, it had most of the elements of the ancient cathedral office, so long lost in the West: prayer and praise on a highly repetitious pattern without any compulsion to cover the psalter or all of scripture.

On the surface, it all sounds highly innocuous but beneath it lay one of the roots of a social revolution which is still not complete. In the 1830s it became common, especially in western New York, to encourage women to pray aloud in the mid-week prayer meeting. This scandalized more conservative clergy from New England. In 1835, Charles G. Finney summarized these critics: "Set women to praying? Why, the next thing, I suppose, will be to set them to preaching."[13] Precisely. Women soon found that their voices could be heard not just in prayer meetings, not only in church, but in an array of social crusades. The first Women's Rights Convention met in a Wesleyan (anti-slavery) Methodist Church in Seneca Falls, New York in 1848. The mid-week prayer meeting gave women a voice in public for the first time except for the limited circles of Quaker meetings. With improving transportation in frontier regions, farmers could sell their crops for cash and purchase factory-made cloth, thus emancipating their wives from the half of their labor which had gone into spinning and weaving. The new leisure could be devoted to religion and social causes. The prayer meeting led the way. It was social dynamite.

In thousands of homes, daily family prayers have continued down to the present. These have been reinforced by the continuing production of manuals, prayerbooks, and other sources. A good example of this genre is *A Manual of Family Worship with an Essay on the Christian Family* by the Reverend J. S. Mills and Professor J. H. Ruebush, published in 1900.[14] It consists of select poems, scriptures, select hymns, and sacred songs. Today, various denominational periodicals function in a similar fashion.

The Eucharist

For most Christians, the eucharist has remained the very heart and center of Christian worship. Yet there have been major shifts in both practice and belief in modern times.

As we have indicated, the Enlightenment mentality took a dim view of sacraments in general and of the eucharist in particular. By and large, Roman Catholicism reacted to the Enlightenment by ignoring it. A few exceptions only prove the rule. Under Bishop Scipione DeRicci, the Synod of Pistoia of 1786 attempted a number of reforms in northern Italy; all were quickly quashed by Rome.[15] Catholic sacramental theology tended to focus in this period on the concept of validity, i.e., what is necessary, sometimes the minimal, for the assurance of a genuine work of grace. This gave the appearance of reducing the sacraments to a mechanical efficiency which bordered on magic. Catholic theology was more concerned with the sacraments as effecting grace rather than as signifying it. For people of the Enlightenment, this meant a real split from the thought modes of the rest of life.

The effects of the Enlightenment were much more powerful in most of Protestantism where the eucharist came to be seen largely as a memorial which we keep because Christ demanded we do so. One Anglican bishop could even suggest that the words "in remembrance" meant that Christ was not present.[16] That caused something of a furor at the time (1735) but Bishop Hoadly spoke for many and the concept of the Lord's Supper as basically a wake became and remains very prevalent. In essence, the eucharist was moralized: "If Jesus could die for you, why cannot you live righteously?" The essence of thousands of communion sermons continues to be: "Jesus died; Be good." This is certainly the predominant view in much of American Protestantism (and at the popular level probably in much of Roman Catholicism). And it is perfectly in accord with the Enlightenment tenet that religion's chief purpose is to be morally edifying.

Early Methodism reacted against the Enlightenment by viewing the eucharist as a means of grace in which the presence of

Christ is experienced. John and Charles Wesley published in 1745 *Hymns on the Lord's Supper*,[17] a collection of 166 eucharistic hymns, the greatest such treasury in the English language. They get beyond the negativism about sacrifice of the Reformation period, depict the means of the presence of Christ in the eucharist as a mystery, describe the eucharist as the work of the Spirit, and emphasize the eschatological dimension. John Wesley preached on the necessity of constant (i.e., frequent) communion which in his own life meant about twice a week. But little of this eucharistic piety survived him.

The next eucharistic revival came on the American Frontier. The followers of Barton W. Stone and Alexander Campbell became convinced that the biblical record decreed a weekly eucharist. As Campbell wrote: "A cloud of witnesses to the plainness and evidence of the New Testament on the subject of the weekly celebration of the Lord's Supper might be adduced."[18] His followers in the backwoods of Kentucky formed the Christian Church (Disciples of Christ) in 1832 and even since have practiced a weekly eucharist with the whole community receiving communion. Soon thereafter, the new Mormon movement accepted a weekly eucharist as did the Plymouth Brethren in England.

What had begun in the backwoods of Kentucky was soon to be replicated in the halls of Canterbury. The Catholic Revival in the Church of England, although initiated as a reaction to lost clerical power and influence in the national government, soon became a major revival of the eucharist. From three times a year, it eventually became the main Sunday service for most Anglicans, with all communing. What began in Oxford had little connection with ceremonial at first but the Cambridge Movement led to a revival of much of the ceremonial absent for centuries in the English church. Medievalism was in vogue and although no words of the prayerbook were changed, just about every other aspect of Anglican worship was. Vestments, candles and a cross on the altar-table, stone altars, incense, the presider with his back to the congregation, the mixed chalice, all these and more were revived, centuries after they had been discarded by Anglicans. Movements calling for placing the eucharist once again at the center of worship were underway in Danish and German Lutheranism. They looked to restoring what was normative for Luther.

The onset of the twentieth century saw a major change in Roman Catholic practice. The mass had remained unchanged in text since 1570 but Pope Pius X initiated a movement that led Catholics to receive frequent communion. The medieval practice of infrequent communion which still persisted was finally overcome although habits such as giving communion before or after mass survived until Vatican II. Pius also encouraged greater participation by encouraging the laity to pray (silently) the mass and to sing portions in Gregorian chant.

The pace of change picked up considerably after the Second Vatican Council (1962–1965). The period after World War II had seen Pope Pius XII's rather conservative encyclical, *Mediator Dei* of 1947, give recognition to the liturgical movement. But a second liturgical movement was already underway in North America and Europe, with strong pressure for the mass in the vernacular, for a new emphasis on scripture, and increased participation by the laity. The *Constitution on the Sacred Liturgy* (1963) of Vatican II encouraged many of these tendencies without realizing how far they might go.

Under the leadership of Pope Paul VI, many changes went forward during the late 1960s. These resulted eventually in the entire mass being translated into the various languages of the world, the structure of the mass being returned to that of the early church, and, for the first time in the Roman rite, four eucharistic prayers in place of the single one. Preaching was to occur at every Sunday mass, the altar-tables were moved so the priest could celebrate facing the people, and congregational song encouraged. An Old Testament reading, psalmody, and intercessory prayers were restored and much ceremonial that no longer was meaningful removed.

Pastoral discretion was given a higher role and priests had to choose from a variety of possible options. At first, gestures to indigenization were made but Rome became increasingly apprehensive about losing control and, with the exception of an African mass for Zaire, control has remained increasingly rigid with Rome

overriding the pleas of national hierarchies for further inculturation.

A major shift has come about in new understandings of
sacramentality in which the focus is on the human recipient and
the means by which humans perceive reality. This has meant that
the sacraments, and particularly the eucharist, have been rein-
terpreted with emphasis on how they signify. For the first time,
the human sciences have been mined to understand how humans
relate to each other. On a pastoral level, this means that the
quality of celebration has become of prime concern. Concretely,
that is expressed in the use of real bread, in the giving of the cup
to the laity, and in celebrating while facing the people. Many of
the devotions which once occupied the people while the lonely
priest said the mass have been pushed aside for a greater sense of
corporate involvement in offering thanksgiving together.

Many of the Roman Catholic trends have been reflected in
mainline Protestant churches. Indeed, the new rites look so much
alike that one needs to read the hymnal cover to see what church
one is in. The official eucharistic rites of the Roman Catholic,
Lutheran, Anglican, Reformed, and Methodist traditions are very
similar. That does not mean that the style of celebration is the
same although that can vary tremendously within traditions. Anglicans use real wine while Methodists use real bread. These
idiosyncrasies are not minor, but the shape of the liturgy has
certainly coalesced.

For many Christians in the Frontier and Pentecostal Traditions, little has changed. These groups usually give the highest
value to pastoral discretion which means the wording of most of
the service, including the eucharistic prayer, is composed locally.
Although many mainline churches have moved to more frequent
communion, this is far from universal. Some groups such as most
English Pentecostals have a weekly eucharist; others may feel four
times a year is sufficient. Seventh-Day Adventists speak of the
"thirteenth Sabbath" communion dividing the year precisely into
quarters. Thus for many American Protestants, the eucharist is an
occasional service, more infrequent than baptisms in many cases.

The Preaching Service

At this point we must introduce a new category for which there is no standard name. It is called simply Sunday service, the service of the word, or morning order. The chief limitation is that it is not the eucharist and we have chosen the dominant feature, preaching. The *Westminster Directory* calls it simply "Public Worship of God" and it became the norm for much of English-speaking Reformed and Puritan Traditions.

There are three possible sources for this type of service. In one sense it derives from Anglican morning prayer with the addition of a sermon. This would seem most likely in the Methodist Tradition. A typical Methodist *Discipline*, that of 1844, simply instructs: "Let the morning service consist of singing, prayer, the reading of a chapter out of the Old Testament, and another out of the New and preaching."[19] The first prayer was to conclude with the Lord's Prayer and the whole service with the apostolic benediction (II Cor. 13:13). The reference to both testaments seems more in line with morning prayer than the eucharist.

A second possible source is the Reformed Tradition's use of the service of the word from the eucharist as the model. This always included a sermon. For English-speaking Protestantism, this had been tempered in the *Westminster Directory* of 1645 which gave the sequence: call to worship, prayer, scripture ("ordinarily one chapter of each testament"), the long prayer, sermon, prayer after the sermon, the singing of a psalm, and dismissal "with a solemn blessing."

The third source, which still prevails in many churches, derives from the peculiar conditions of the frontier where there were large numbers of unchurched people. The most effective form of ministry to a widely-scattered population, most of whom had no church affiliation, developed in Kentucky in the form of the camp meeting. Gaspar River in 1800 and Cane Ridge in 1801 mark the emergence of this type of ministry as a development from the sacramental seasons of the Scots-Irish Presbyterians. The procedure was to call together everyone within fifty miles for several days of preaching, prayer, hymn singing, and spiritual counseling.

Then, new converts would be baptized and the meeting would conclude with the eucharist. Camp meetings were probably our first ecumenical occasions: Methodists, Baptists, Presbyterians, and Disciples of Christ collaborated. They also brought together preachers black and white and both races contributed to the hymnody.

The goal of such meetings was conversion of sinners. And thousands of the unchurched were brought to Christian faith through camp meetings. Writing in 1854, after much of the enthusiasm for the camp meetings had declined, B. W. Gorham declared "Multitudes hear the gospel at Camp Meetings who rarely or never attend church services elsewhere; and of these attracted to the place as they have been, by the singularity of the occasion, thousands have been converted to God. Nor are these the only souls converted at Camp Meeting. These meetings are perhaps never held without being attended by persons under a painful sense of unforgiven sin, and who go there . . . to avail themselves of the extraordinary facilities there afforded for seeking salvation."[20]

These frontier patterns, a generation later, were transmitted to the more settled east coast. More than any other individual, Charles G. Finney, a Presbyterian minister turned Congregationalist with a Methodist theology, was instrumental in domesticating practices developed on the frontier for east coast Protestant worship. Finney's new measures were not original but well practiced in the West. He would certainly squirm at being called the greatest liturgical reformer of the nineteenth century but he probably influenced the worship life of more people than anyone else of that century. Finney operated on a fierce pragmatism; tradition is of no importance. Whatever works in worship should be used for even "our present forms of public worship . . . have been arrived at by degrees, and by a succession of new measures."[21]

The result was a reshaping of American worship in line with the Frontier Tradition. This affected greatly the Methodist, Reformed, and Puritan Traditions, to a lesser degree the Lutheran Tradition, and even (in the West) the Quaker Tradition. It led to a homogeneity in Sunday morning worship in many of these traditions but was resisted by the Anglican Tradition and escaped much contact with the Anabaptist Tradition. The consequence is a three-part Sunday service modeled on revival techniques originally developed in camp meetings. The first part is a service of prayer and praise which includes considerable musical elements. Congregational singing developed and choirs were introduced. Extempore prayer was offered. And a lesson was read, usually a single lesson, as the basis for the sermon. The second part was fervent preaching which was the major event of the service (and for which all else sometimes seemed preparatory). The sermon called the unconverted to conversion, sinners to repentance, and the godly to rejoice in their salvation. The third part was a harvest of those converted or those recommitting their lives to Jesus Christ.

The pattern has proved remarkably durable. It still forms the outline of most Protestant worship in North America and has spread rapidly in mission areas overseas. What the nineteenth century could not envision, of course, was that this type of worship also works remarkably well as television worship. The choirs have become bigger and the preachers (some of them) a bit more polished, but it is the same frontier pattern now appearing in the homes of unchurched and churched alike via electronic technology. Surveys show that thirty per cent of the audience are Roman Catholics. There is obviously a conjunction of this form of worship and profound human needs.

Christian Time

Many changes occurred over this period in the perception and use of time in Christian worship. For Roman Catholics, several major festivals were given universal significance: in 1708, the Feast of the Immaculate Conception became obligatory on a universal scale; the Feast of the Sacred Heart was made a universal obligation in 1856; and at the conclusion of a jubilee year in 1925, Christ the King was instituted.

The other main development (before 1970) was the constant addition of saints as each succeeding century reaped its own harvest or added forgotten saints from previous centuries. Between 1568 and 1960, 171 more saints' commemorations were added to an already crowded calendar. Such holy congestion certainly caused problems, especially in the daily office. Pope Pius X made a piecemeal reform of the breviary in 1912, asserting the prominence of Sunday over all but the greatest feasts.

Vatican II led to the most drastic and systematic reform of the calendar in the history of the Roman communion. Indeed, its merits have commended themselves to many Protestant churches though some keep seasons after Epiphany and Pentecost rather than the more radical step of calling these times "ordinary time." The new *Roman Calendar* went into effect with the beginning of the liturgical year 1970. It reasserted the dominance of Sunday as the chief feast day. The Christmas and Easter cycles have become more distinct with the Easter Triduum (beginning on the evening of Maundy Thursday through Easter vespers) clearly the climax of the whole year. The Sunday after Epiphany is designated the Baptism of the Lord, and Christ the King was moved to the end of the year. The saints' cycle has been simplified and categorized as solemnities, feasts, and memorials. Most of the latter are optional; only saints of worldwide significance must be commemorated; national and regional saints may also receive attention.

The Puritan Tradition had a strong distaste for the observance of the church year other than a strict keeping of Sundays plus occasional days of thanksgiving or fasting. It is significant that many of Charles Wesley's hymns were written for the great festivals of the year: "Hark! the Herald Angels Sing" or "Christ the Lord Is Risen Today," for example. John Wesley, on the other hand, purged the calendar of most of what few holy days were left in the Anglican version "as at present answering no valuable end." Of the thirty-nine special days in the 1662 prayerbook, he retained only six: Christmas Day, Good Friday, Easter Day, Ascension Day, Whit Sunday, and Trinity Sunday.

A century after Charles Wesley, John Keble heralded the Catholic Revival in the Church of England with his collection of poems, *The Christian Year* (1827). The movement itself opted for a much more careful observance of the existing Anglican calendar. Meanwhile, most of the American churches were unconsciously developing a pragmatic calendar of parish and family life. This became a yearly cycle consisting of Mother's Day, the revival, homecoming Sunday, rally day (for the Sunday School), World Communion Sunday, Loyalty Sunday (for pledges), and the inevitable Christmas pageant. These events encapsulated much of what was important in church and family life.

The late nineteenth century and early twentieth century show a slow recovery of the traditional Christian calendar. Heather Murray Elkins has described the often overlooked role of women, the conscientious members of altar guilds, who fostered more careful observances of the festivals.[22] Many churches joined with the Federal Council of Churches in promoting the Christian year on an ecumenical basis. A new season, reflecting the social gospel, was added, "Kingdomtide," but eventually only Methodists retained it.[23]

Since Vatican II, many traditions, even left wing ones, have taken the traditional church year much more seriously. To a considerable extent, this is the result of widespread adoption of versions of the new Roman Catholic Sunday lectionary. Since a lectionary of necessity is built upon a calendar, those who opted for lectionary use found they had also purchased a fuller church year. In 1983, *The Common Lectionary* came into widespread use in much of North America and the South Pacific, and the *Revised Common Lectionary* did so nine years later. Both versions are based on "The Common Calendar" and show a coalescence across a wide spectrum of Protestant worship traditions. The last Sunday after the Epiphany is kept as the Transfiguration; otherwise most of the calendar is familiar, indeed most of it would have been familiar in the late fourth century except for All Saints' Day and Christ the King. A considerable segment of American Protestantism keeps only Christmas and Easter, the pragmatic local church year, plus occasional communion Sundays.

Pastoral Rites

During modern times the pastoral rites have undergone profound changes. A new science, psychology, has led to a clearer understanding of some of the issues in people's lives at these crisis points. To this has been added the studies of cultural anthropology, not to mention deeper awareness of the factors within the history of the Christian tradition in shaping current rites. All have led to profound rethinking of the forms and intentions of the pastoral rites.

1. Reconciliation. Penance disappeared sooner or later in all the Reformation churches except for the practice of the ban still kept by the Anabaptist Tradition. The work of penance was subsumed by general confessions tacked onto Sunday worship and it cast a long shadow over the eucharist. In the eighteenth century, members of the Wesleyan bands were asked each week: "What known sins have you committed since our last meeting? . . . Have you nothing you desire to keep secret?"[24] The recovery of penance as a separate rite began in the Catholic Revival in the Church of England as auricular confession to a priest. Its re-introduction was a source of protest for fear that priests might abuse such intrusion into women's secrets. Only a portion of Anglicanism practices confession to a priest. All churches, on the other hand, have developed pastoral counseling into a major component of ordained ministry although without a liturgical rite.

For Roman Catholics, the norm until recently was confession in a confessional booth to a priest, the receiving of absolution, and the prescribing of a satisfaction. The result of the Post-Vatican II revisions of the ritual has been to provide three quite different possibilities for this sacrament. The first is for individuals but, unlike previous practice, it now often takes place face-to-face in a reconciliation room. The second is with a group of penitents and begins with a service of the word and general confession before individual confession and absolution. The third, whose use has been increasingly limited, is similar through the general confession but then absolution is pronounced in general.[25] In actual practice, confession has become much less common while communion at mass has increased.

2. Healing. For Roman Catholics, this sacrament has probably changed more than any other. Up to recent times, the *Roman Ritual* of 1614 was followed in Latin and the American translation only came out in 1954. The *Constitution on the Sacred Liturgy* pointed out that the familiar name, "Extreme Unction," was less appropriate than calling it "'anointing of the sick,' [since it] is not a sacrament for those only who are at the point of death."[26] The change of a name is often a sign of a major change in a reality, and that certainly is true in this case. It has been rethought as a sacrament of healing, much in line with early Christian practice. Anointing may be repeated and is clearly linked with life and health rather than death alone. For the dying, a continuous rite of confession, anointing, and viaticum is provided.

The Protestant appropriation of this sacrament begins with the Church of the Brethren, a German pietist group of the early eighteenth century resembling in many ways the Anabaptists. They simply took seriously James 5 and began anointing with oil for the purpose of healing and have continued this practice. This was probably the first Protestant use of anointing for any purpose since 1552 although sickroom communions continued to be common. In the nineteenth century, healing became important in two churches loosely reflecting the Frontier Tradition in worship. Both were led by women who had suffered ill health. Mary Baker Eddy founded Christian Science and placed great emphasis on faith as the principal healer. Ellen Gould White, co-founder of the Seventh Day Adventist Church stressed a ministry of healing, largely through diet and exercise.

It was the Pentecostal Tradition that recovered healing in public worship as one of many gifts of the Holy Spirit. Many Pentecostal churches have healing as a regular part of Sunday worship. The healers are usually lay members of the congregation who pray and lay hands on those needing healing. These gifts have been particularly apparent in some of the new independent African churches where healing is a cherished gift.

3. Christian Marriage. Quite naturally, marriage rites tend to be the most conservative since society has so much at stake in the process. The Reformation rites drew largely on the existing milieu and the Roman Catholic *Ritual* of 1614 codified Roman practices without enforcing them. John Wesley eliminated the giving away of the bride for reasons unknown and also the exchange of rings (in accord with Puritan objections to it). American Methodists eventually restored both, but in 1864 and 1910 did remove the bride's vow to obey.[27]

Marriage rites throughout history have yielded to largely secular pressures to be fashion and flower shows and social events.

One is never quite certain whether when, after fifteen hundred years it came inside the church, it was worth the effort to get it there or not. The actual rite changed little over most of this period except on some occasions to become more conservative.

The post–Vatican II rites again mirror social changes but also show some distinct Christian witness. The blatant inequality of the Roman Catholic rite with a prayer for the woman that she be "faithful to one embrace, . . . honorable in her chastity" with no similar concern for the man has been changed. Most of the new rites stress the equality of partners, making the giving away of the bride especially problematic.

The new rites are designed specifically as Christian worship with elements of congregational participation such as hymns, psalms, and prayers. Some invite congregational affirmations to uphold the couple. Many now provide for a nuptial eucharist. This becomes a problem in mixed marriages but is becoming increasingly common among Protestants. An indication of the commonality of the new wedding rites is the publication by the Consultation on Common Texts of *A Christian Celebration of Marriage: An Ecumenical Liturgy*.[28] Although the American Catholic bishops have sought its use, the Vatican has not yet agreed. But it does show how similar the various rites have become. Those churches outside the ecumenical orbit often shape wedding services at pastoral discretion which frequently means borrowing from churches that have set services of marriage.

4. Christian Burial. This, too, has largely been governed by secular society, showing an ever increasing level of affluence. Before the seventeenth century, ordinary people did not merit tombstones; coffins for them became common in the nineteenth century, as did embalming after the Civil War in the United States, although not in most of the West. Eventually the disposal of the dead was left to secular businesses who spoke of the undertaking profession.

Burial rites have long consisted essentially of reiteration of the scriptural promises in the forms of psalms, prayers, and scripture readings. For Roman Catholics, a requiem mass might be celebrated but the context showed a great preoccupation with the sinfulness of the deceased.

The rites since Vatican II show a new orientation to focus on the paschal mystery of the resurrected Christ. The shift from black vestments to white, i.e., from despair to hope, signifies the drastic reorientation that has occurred in both Protestant and Catholic funerals. The newest Catholic rite for the United States, the 1989 *Order of Christian Funerals*,[29] shows a maximum of flexibility in adapting to changing pastoral situations. Some Protestant churches now provide for the possibility of the eucharist at funerals. Out of the music performed at black funerals has grown an important musical idiom. The twin functions of consolation of the bereaved and committal of the deceased are handled in a variety of ways in different parts of the country and in various segments of society. Funerals probably reflect as much social diversity as any form of worship.

LIVING TOGETHER IN COMMUNITY

Leadership

Questions of leadership have confronted each new movement in Christianity. Changes have also come about in ancient churches, sometimes when least expected. For Roman Catholics, the *Roman Pontifical* of 1596 dictated the rites for ordination until quite recently. But in 1972 the centuries-old minor orders and subdiaconate were dropped and men (only) instituted as readers and acolytes. The ambiguity about bishops was removed by renaming the rite "Ordination of a Bishop." Even more important, the emphasis shifted away from seeing ministry in terms of power and authority to service of community. The ordination rites of the new *Roman Pontifical* were approved by Paul VI in 1972. They emphasize ordination by invocation of the Holy Spirit to pour out the requisite gifts necessary for each order of ministry. The *Apostolic Tradition* has provided the model.

Each of the traditions originating in this period began under different circumstances. John Wesley believed that presbyters and bishops were essentially the same order but with different functions. He also held firmly that the eucharist was essential to the church and that only ordained elders (presbyters) could preside. So he violated church order for the sake of mission and ordained men for ministry even though a priest himself. He provided three ordination rites in his *Sunday Service for the Methodists of North America*[30] of 1784 and his American followers soon took the name bishop for what he had termed "superintendant." Wesley also enlisted the help of many lay preachers, some of whom were women. But only the ordained were allowed to minister the sacraments. Indeed, he was more clerical than Roman Catholics on baptism.

The Frontier Tradition in America developed a variety of patterns. The movement that became the Christian Church (Disciples of Christ) was also confronted with presidency at the eucharist. Unlike Wesley (and Schillebeeckx in our time) advocating the conservative method, i.e., make more presbyters, they took the radical solution of allowing lay people to preside. Here was Jacksonian democracy in full liturgical flower. Eighteen hundred years after Christ, lay people were finally allowed to preside at His table. Liturgical democracy had finally arrived in the backwoods of Kentucky. The Mormons developed a somewhat different approach by making most male members priests in a variety of priesthoods.

Another notable development during this period was the appearance of lay evangelists. Dwight L. Moody was the best known but women could and did enter this ministry, most notably Phoebe Palmer, long before the ordained ministry was open to them. Paradoxically, it was the rather conservative Holiness churches, putting aside I Corinthians 14:34, which first began to ordain women. A century later, this had become common in most Protestant churches other than Missouri Synod Lutherans. Women played a leading role in forming some of the Pentecostal churches.

In the Pentecostal Tradition, a firm link was made between the gift of the Holy Spirit and ordination. Only those who could give evidence of the baptism of the Spirit and the bestowal of its gifts could receive ordination. The rite operates more or less as congregational ratification of what the Spirit already has done.

In the Catholic Revival in the Church of England, a reaction to the loss of power and prestige in civil life led to a new affirmation of the dignity and power of ordained ministry. This was reflected in church architecture, as one contemporary wrote, by building chancels to show the necessary separation of clergy from their flock. A new clericalism developed in Anglicanism at the same time the Frontier Tradition was finally overcoming it. In 1896, for largely political reasons, Pope Leo XIII condemned Anglican orders as "absolutely null and utterly void" because of presumed defects in form and intention.[31]

Since Vatican II, there has been considerable convergence in ordination rites since everyone basically is borrowing from the *Apostolic Tradition*. The secondary ceremonies of the medieval period have receded from prominence and most rites suggest congregational approval, examination of candidates, a homily, prayer invoking the Spirit with laying on of hands, handing over of symbolic instruments or Bibles, and the celebration of the eucharist.

There is also a general inclination to see ordained ministry in the context of the ministry of all the baptized. The move away from power and control to service is clear. Still, the theological and sociological problems are severe. *Baptism, Eucharist and Ministry* shows the perplexities that still hound ecumenical discussions of these issues.[32] Not the least of these remains the ordination of women. The Orthodox, or some of them, now seem more flexible on this than the present Roman Catholic administration.

Most exciting are the developments of base communities in Latin America which have accomplished the reinvention of the Church in an effort "to conceptualize the church more from the foundation up than from the steeple down."[33] Such new thinking comes as a serious challenge to views that see the church as synonymous with the hierarchy. Protestant communities in Latin America seem even more successful in drawing leadership roles from within local communities rather than imposing it from "above."[34]

Preaching

By all accounts, the modern period is one of great prominence for preaching of the word. A variety of movements from American revivalism to the Catholic Revival in the Church of England was promoted by means of distinguished preachers. New styles of preaching developed to fit each social situation.

In the eighteenth century, John Wesley and George Whitefield "transformed the function of the pulpit and also the religious life of England and North America."[35] At a time when the average Anglican sermon consisted largely of "fifteen minutes doses of morality," Wesley and Whitefield took to the streets and fields to bring their message to the unchurched masses, many of them former country folk dislocated by the industrial revolution and enclosure of common lands. Their message was the glad tidings of salvation preached in a direct and down-to-earth fashion. Wesley was essentially the Oxford don and Whitefield the actor. Davies summarizes them as Wesley having "more light than heat" and Whitefield "more heat than light." But in any case, they developed evangelical preaching. This had been foreshadowed in the Great Awakening preachers in America, Jonathan Edwards, Gilbert Tennent, and others. In effect, the English evangelists were reaching a new audience, those who had never darkened the door of a church. Field preaching became an important recovery of what the apostolic church and the mendicant friars had practiced but which had been forgotten in an age of gentility.

Many of these patterns persisted in nineteenth-century preaching in America. The Second Great Awakening brought its share of distinguished preachers: Barton W. Stone, Alexander Campbell, Francis Asbury, Charles G. Finney, Timothy Dwight, and Lyman Beecher, representing a variety of traditions. Many of them traveled widely, preaching wherever they could gain an audience. Some of them featured highly emotional appeals; others were more restrained. Black preachers came to share in camp meetings and sometimes served predominantly white congregations.

A new phenomenon came to be the traveling revivalist of whom Finney was the most notable but Dwight L. Moody, Billy Sunday, Sam Jones, Billy Graham, and many others right down to the present became national figures. Unfortunately, revivalism became a system just as the sacraments had in the scholastic period and sometimes became too professional and slick.

The effect in local churches was to produce princes of the pulpit whose sermons dominated worship and excluded much response except for those converted who would troop down the aisle to be baptized. The architectural impact is visible; relatively small tub or wineglass pulpits were replaced by pulpit platforms and a desk pulpit which scarcely confined energetic preachers as they pleaded for conversions. It is not strange that television in our time should be a natural vehicle for this style of preaching which was initially conceived to reach the unchurched and to reheat the fires of those who had grown lukewarm. Even Roman Catholic priests in America felt the need for revival missions: "revival religion not only found a home in the Catholic community, it also became the most popular religious experience of Catholic Americans in the second half of the nineteenth century."[36]

But this was by no means the only style of preaching in the previous century. Much of the appeal of the Catholic Revival in the Church of England came through the preaching of John Henry Newman and E. B. Pusey. Newman in his early years had been influenced by the English evangelicals, the greatest of whom was Charles Simeon of Cambridge. And in the great middle-ground Broad Church-party preaching was at its best in Frederick W. Robertson of Brighton. Charles H. Spurgeon, a Baptist, reigned supreme as the most influential English preacher and teacher of preachers. A great succession of English preachers, both Anglican and Free Church followed in their footsteps. The so-called Free Church conscience was often articulated in sermons dealing with social issues.

In America, the Social Gospel was largely promoted by sermons on social topics. The names of Washington Gladden, Walter Rauschenbusch, and Frank Mason North became associated with the new approach to preaching. Harry Emerson Fosdick led the crusade against fundamentalism, largely from the pulpit. Topical preaching came into prominence in the liberal churches of this era and preaching "to real life situations" tended to take precedence over biblical preaching.

Recent years have seen a new concern for preaching in all churches of the West. Considerable efforts have gone into improving the quality of preaching in Roman Catholic churches now that it is mandatory at Sunday masses. In turn, many mainline churches have invested deeply in lectionary preaching which has had the consequence of turning away from the topical to the exegetical mode. Preaching is more closely integrated into the rest of the service so that one can again speak of liturgical preaching. This is by no means universal; many of the evangelical churches have kept their own course with preaching that may be biblical but often is neither exegetical nor liturgical. The black churches provide steady testimony to the power of the preached word in reshaping lives. Congregational exclamations of agreement and support give an additional dimension of participation.

Church Music

The changes in church music have been equally profound in this period. We have seen the English Puritan Tradition just beginning to open up to the possibility of singing "uninspired," i.e., non-scriptural, hymns under the leadership of Isaac Watts. This burst into full bloom with Charles Wesley who wrote over 6,500 hymns, many of which are still popular today. Frequently he turned theological treatises or devotional reading into poetry. The doctrinal content of his hymns is high and the eucharistic hymns are our best source for Wesleyan eucharistic doctrine.

A gigantic figure for church music during the eighteenth century was Johann Sebastian Bach (1685–1750). In a straightforward workmanlike way, he composed music faithfully following the traditional Lutheran lectionary for his parish in Leipzig. The services were largely musical in the form of sung ordinary parts and cantatas on the lessons. In addition to choral music, he wrote magnificent organ works and the pietism of the era finds expression in his passion music. Bach's music shows just how ecumenical music is; it is used throughout the western liturgical traditions.

The nineteenth century brought major changes in all types of church music. Hymnody turned more and more to the subjective. Much of the music of the frontier focused on how one felt about God, not on what God has done for us. The first person pronoun loomed large in this hymnody of feeling. In this process, black and white spirituals mingled as means of expressing one's journey to the promised land.

The Frontier Tradition was not slow in realizing how valuable choral music was as part of the service of prayer and praise. Churches added solos, duets, trios, quartets, and octets as the choral resources increased. The choir, once avoided by Puritans and Methodists alike, came to be a staple of much worship. Music was often used in a frankly manipulative way in preparing people to be receptive to gospel preaching.

At the same time, but for quite different reasons, choirs were being introduced into English parish churches. Choirs of monks were not available but lay people were vested as clerics and used to fill the new or restored chancels. The period saw a growing attendance at evensong, now largely sung by choirs. At the same time, John Mason Neale and others led a movement to introduce hymn singing into Anglican churches. He took the lead in translating medieval texts, despite objections to hymn singing as "Methodistical snuffling." These hymns are noted for their objective recital of salvation history, often written for occasions of the church year.

Roman Catholicism saw the recovery of Gregorian chant, at first in the newly reconstituted monasteries, eventually in parish churches. Much of this was a deliberate rebuff to the highly operatic service music of composers such as Rossini, music that usually demanded professional singers. Part of the appeal of the chant was its association with earlier ages of piety but it was also vigorously promoted by Pope Pius X as a means of participation by the laity in singing in Latin the ordinary parts of the mass.[37] In retrospect, strenuous efforts to bring this about seem like a good run down the wrong road.

After Vatican II, this effort was supplanted by the development of congregational hymnody sung to music of the present and recent centuries. Today's hymnals borrow indiscriminately from whatever tradition seems to have produced something of value. Catholics are almost as likely to sing "Amazing Grace" as are Protestants; the St. Louis Jesuits appear in most new Protestant hymnals.

In the late nineteenth century hymn writing took an even more subjective basis. The most distinguished writer was a blind woman, Fanny J. Crosby, who was revered as a saint at the time. A black minister, Charles A. Tindley, began writing gospel songs. His mantle was inherited by Thomas A. Dorsey, writer of "Precious Lord, Take My Hand." And gospel songs and the blues became a significant contribution from the black churches.[38] Modern hymnals may be our most democratic books; they try to reflect a cross section of our society. The worship music of minorities and the white majority appear on facing pages, a mirror to the cultural diversity of our times.

Church Architecture

Once again, the building of churches reflects and summarizes much that has gone on in modern times. From the onset, the Americas provided a vast laboratory for designing liturgical architecture to fit new concepts of worship. The Roman Catholic missionaries tended to replicate much familiar in their homelands. Where they were Jesuits, the centralized nature of the order often meant that baroque style churches were built according to plans sent out from or approved in Rome. But Jesuits were also sensitive to native architecture where it existed, as in New Mexico, and provided early examples of architectural inculturation. But by and large an international style of baroque architecture emerged. These featured altar-tables before a dramatic reredos, communion rails, a pulpit in the nave (often without pews), a font usually in a niche at the entrance, and a balcony for choirs.

In the course of the eighteenth century, a characteristic building type, sometimes referred to as the "Protestant plain style" emerged in the Puritan meetinghouse. But by the end of the century, new architectural sophistication coming from England had reoriented these so the pulpit was at the end of a short side, opposite an entrance with tower and portico. These replaced buildings with the pulpit in the center of a long side opposite a single entrance. Quakers built meetinghouses with a movable partition so the sexes could meet separately or together. A wide variety of experiments was tried by Anglicans.[39] Many centered around a triple-decker pulpit, reading desk, and clerk's desk. The altar-table could appear in a variety of locations, sometimes opposite the pulpit; the font was usually at the church entrance.

Major changes came in the nineteenth century. The Frontier Tradition favored a pulpit platform, often with three chairs: for the preacher, the visiting preacher, and the song leader. A desk pulpit in front and a banked choir behind became the normal arrangement for this concert stage arrangement. The Akron plan, so popular after 1870, focused all this in a corner, surrounded by concentric pews on a sloping floor. The advent of the Sunday school had major impact on church architecture. It demanded an assembly space for "opening exercises," i.e., children's worship, and separate classrooms. Many churches were altered to accommodate these new needs.

In England, a major crusade began in the 1840s to restore existing medieval churches to their late medieval arrangement and to build new churches after the patterns of the fourteenth century. Triggered by a Roman Catholic, A. W. N. Pugin, the gothic revival had few successes in persuading Roman Catholics but Anglicans lapped it up. A distinct Anglican church type, modeled on a medieval village church, with a long chancel, a remote altar-table, and full of medieval ornaments, was found all over England. The chief proponents were a group of Cambridge undergraduates banded together as the Cambridge Camden Society.[40] They researched medieval churches, restored many to a "correct" form, and pressured architects to imitate approved medieval models. And these buildings spread all over the globe. From Copenhagen to Tasmania, it was easy to spot an Anglican church until quite recently.

A new era began slowly in this century with Frank Lloyd Wright building the first modern church in Oak Park, Illinois, in 1905. Modern architecture caught on very slowly, partly because the second gothic revival, led in the United States by Ralph Adams Cram, produced so many notable examples that everyone tried to imitate.

Two German architects, Dominikus Böhm and Rudolf Schwarz, led the way to reflecting the German liturgical movement in their architecture. After World War II necessitated the rebuilding of so many churches, they provided leadership in a new

Catholic church architecture. They are ascetic, the focus is entirely on the liturgical action, and there are few, if any, devotional objects present.

One of the most immediate effects of Vatican II was the (First) *Instruction on Implementing the Constitution on the Sacred Liturgy* which appeared September 26, 1964. This mandated moving the altar-table to a free-standing position so the priest could face the people across it. This led to many changes: removal of side altar-tables, moving the tabernacle, a more prominent pulpit (or ambo), a presidential chair so the priest could sit down and delegate portions of the mass to a variety of ministers, and the wholesale destruction of much art that had provided for personal devotions. So ascetic are many of these churches that one can now speak of a "Catholic plain style." The most recent change has been the slow introduction of baptistries where both infants and adults can be baptized by immersion.

Many of the same changes have been echoed in remodeled or newly-built mainline Protestant churches. The font is usually located near the pulpit and altar-table since baptism is always public. The presidential chair is often less prominent, partly because of memories of the ugliness of earlier pulpit chairs. Many evangelical churches are built around a central pulpit. In denominations where believers' baptism is practiced by immersion, the baptistery is a large pool at the front of the church, usually concealed by a curtain when not in use. The architectural problems of dealing with a baptismal pool are daunting.

The earlier iconoclasm of much of Protestantism dates from a time when it was taken seriously that liturgical art had power that could be abused. In the nineteenth century, art began a slow return, usually being used for decorative purposes. But there has been a gradual recovery of liturgical art as an expression of the numinous quality of worship space. For Roman Catholics this has often meant that less is more; for Protestants more may be an improvement. At any rate, our eyes have been opened to the power of the visual to state that which is the object of our worship: God in our midst.

FOR FURTHER READING

Bugnini, Annibale. *The Reform of the Liturgy, 1948–1975.* Matthew J. O'Connell, trans. Collegeville: Liturgical Press, 1990.

Davies, Horton. *Worship and Theology in England.* Princeton: Princeton University Press, 1961–1975. 5 vols.

Documents on the Liturgy, 1963–1979. Collegeville: Liturgical Press, 1982.

Dorgan, Howard. *Giving Glory to God in Appalachia: Worship Practices of Six Baptist Subdenominations.* Knoxville: University of Tennessee Press, 1987.

Hall, Stanley R. "The American Presbyterian Directory for Worship: History of a Liturgical Strategy." Unpublished Ph.D. dissertation, University of Notre Dame, 1990.

Hollenweger, Walter J. *The Pentecostals: The Charismatic Movement in the Churches.* Minneapolis: Augsburg Publishing Company, 1972.

McDonnell, Kilian. *Charismatic Renewal and the Churches.* New York: Seabury Press, 1976.

McLoughlin, William G. *Revivals, Awakenings, and Reform.* Chicago: University of Chicago Press, 1978.

Rattenbury, J. Ernest. *The Eucharistic Hymns of John and Charles Wesley.* Cleveland: O.S.L. Publications, 1991.

Titon, Jeff Todd. *Powerhouse for God: Speech, Chant, and Song in an Appalachian Baptist Church.* Austin: University of Texas Press, 1988.

Wade, William N. "A History of Public Worship in the Methodist Episcopal Church," Unpublished Ph.D. dissertation. University of Notre Dame, 1981.

White, James F. *New Forms of Worship.* Nashville: Abingdon Press, 1971.

CHAPTER VI

Worship in the Churches
of the Future

We have come a long way. Since there is little that we can say about the future with any certainty, this will be a very short chapter. But we can proclaim with confidence some of the things that we have learned which will endure past our times.

The history of Christian worship so far has been an amazing combination of practices and concepts that have remained constant and those that have changed over the course of the centuries. The *Constitution on the Sacred Liturgy* notes that "liturgy is made up of immutable elements divinely instituted, and of elements subject to change. These not only may but ought to be changed with the passage of time if they have suffered from the intrusion of anything out of harmony with the inner nature of the liturgy or have become unsuited to it."[1] It is not always clear in any given time just which is which; only by looking backward do we recognize what has disappeared and what has survived. Some of those things that disappear are recovered in subsequent ages but by no means all of them. That which does survive from age to age seems to have a valid claim to being of genuine value.

Change itself is one of the constants, obviously more rapid in some eras than in others, but never ceasing altogether. Change is a given of any human activity whether it be architecture or handwriting. So it is safe to predict that Christian worship will continue to change, even while retaining some "immutable elements." It may well be that the next chapters in Christian worship will be written in Africa where exciting things in worship seem to be coming to maturity today. Or will it be Korea? Some might suggest Latin America. Or will it be in our midst as new feminist forms of worship come to the forefront? It is not impossible that syncretic traditions of worship will develop as Christians learn to live side by side with other world religions.

The variety of possibilities in any given culture will likely increase. We have seen how a single western tradition was superseded by the Roman Catholic Tradition and nine Protestant traditions. Within many of these traditions is a variety of styles such as Hispanic Pentecostals or Black Catholics. Each is recognizably part of a definite tradition but brings its own cultural contributions, usually most evident in the form of church music. It is exciting to look forward to the development of even more traditions and styles as various groups assert their own social and cultural identities.

Future generations may find the ecumenical consensus document, *Baptism, Eucharist and Ministry*,[2] to be retrogressive. Perhaps we should do more to encourage diversity rather than to seek consensus. We do not yet have enough varieties of Christian worship. What can be done to help liturgically disenfranchised groups to express their worship of the Christian God in forms that are natural to them? How do such groups learn to be themselves in their worship of Jesus Christ?

Increasingly, it seems that efforts by so-called liturgical law to make a single pattern of worship dominate are anachronistic. This may have had its place in the sixteenth century, though even that is dubious, but today such work seems to be a millstone around the necks of Christians. If one sees Christ as in dialogue with culture, then cultures must have a voice, too. Fundamentally, power and control over the worship of others is alien to the genius of Christian worship itself, particularly when exercised on the basis of purely arbitrary authority. The churches exist from the grassroots up and usually liturgical decisions should be made at the lowest level possible. Pastoral discretion has been with us at least since Justin Martyr. It kept Christian worship alive through the heroic age of the martyrs; it still has much to recommend it even in an age of religious prosperity.

The God whom we worship, after all, seems to relish diversity. If no two leaves of grass are the same and certainly no two people identical, then it does not seem strange that there is so much variety in cultures. Our hope is that every culture can learn to name the name of Jesus in its own tongue. Each culture will have its own contribution to make to the totality of Christian worship. Books of this type will have to become much more complex just to give a rough indication of the diversity of possibilities within a worship that nevertheless contains a unity in its essentials.

This should not surprise us since as early as Paul it was expressed that "we do not know how to pray as we ought, but that very Spirit intercedes [for us] with sighs too deep for words." (Rom. 8:26). That Spirit has been active throughout the whole history of Christian worship, interceding for us when we were speechless, teaching us how to pray in ways which, as we have seen, change from time to time and place to place. The liturgy is not the subject of law but of the Spirit, a restless Spirit that keeps prodding the churches forward to new and more eloquent attempts to express that which is "too deep for words."

It is our trust that the Spirit will continue to guide a people otherwise mute in wonder before the love and majesty of God in Jesus Christ into ever new forms of expressing that which is in our hearts. It will change, it will be more varied, and best of all it will be under the guidance of the Holy Spirit who, after all, is God with us. The Spirit has not left us speechless through twenty centuries; it will continue to give us many new voices.

FOR FURTHER READING

Alternative Futures for Worship. Collegeville: Liturgical Press, 1987, 7 volumes.

Chupungco, Anscar J. *Liturgies of the Future: The Process and Methods of Inculturation.* New York: Paulist Press, 1989.

NOTES

Chapter I

1. Wayne A. Meeks, *The First Urban Christians* (New Haven: Yale University Press, 1983) for a survey of thirty individuals about whose social status something can be inferred, pp. 56–63.

2. Ibid., p. 78.

3. Jerome H. Neyrey, ed., *The Social World of Luke-Acts* (Peabody: Hendrickson Publishers, 1991), p. 380.

4. Paul F. Bradshaw, *Daily Prayer in the Early Church* (London: Alcuin Club/S.P.C.K., 1981), p. 25.

5. Joachim Jeremias, *The Eucharistic Words of Jesus* (New York: Charles Scribner's Sons, 1966), p. 125.

6. Ibid., p. 203.

7. Frank Baker, *Methodism and the Love-Feast* (London: Epworth Press, 1957).

8. Thomas J. Talley, "Sources and Structures of the Eucharistic Prayer," *Worship Reforming Tradition* (Washington: Pastoral Press, 1990), p. 17.

9. Cyril C. Richardson, trans. *Early Christian Fathers* (Philadelphia: Westminster Press, 1953), pp. 175–76.

10. Richardson, p. 64.

11. "Philadelphians" 4, Richardson, p. 108.

12. "Ephesians" 20, Richardson, p. 93.

13. Note Geoffrey Wainwright's classic statement of this in *Eucharist and Eschatology* (New York: Oxford University Press, 1981).

14. "Magnesians" 9, Richardson, 96.

15. "Orders and Ordination in the New Testament," *The Study of Liturgy* (New York: Oxford University Press, 1978), p. 293n.

16. "Magnesians" 6, Richardson, p. 95.

17. Gerhard Delling, *Worship in the New Testament* (Philadelphia: Westminster Press, 1962), p. 99.

18. Johannes Quasten, *Music and Worship in Pagan and Christian Antiquity* (Washington: Pastoral Press, 1983), pp. 72-73.

19. Richardson, p. 89.

20. L. Edward Phillips, "The Ritual Kiss in Early Christian Worship," (Unpublished Ph.D. dissertation, University of Notre Dame, 1992), pp. 43-50.

Chapter II

1. Allan Bouley, *From Freedom to Formula* (Washington: Catholic University of America Press, 1981).

2. Geoffrey J. Cuming, *Hippolytus: A Text for Students* (Bramcote: Grove Books, 1976), p. 14. Many of these texts are also found in James F. White, *Documents of Christian Worship* (Louisville: Westminster/John Knox Press, 1992).

3. Anscar J. Chupungco, *Liturgies of the Future: The Process and Methods of Inculturation* (New York: Paulist Press, 1989), p. 37.

4. Marie Conn, trans. text in Cyrille Vogel, *Medieval Liturgy* (Washington: Pastoral Press, 1986), p. 372.

5. Edward Rochie Hardy, trans., *Early Christian Fathers*, edited by Cyril C. Richardson (Philadelphia: Westminster Press, 1953), p. 282.

6. Ernest Evans, trans. *Tertullian's Homily on Baptism* (London: S.P.C.K., 1964), p. 35.

7. R. Hugh Connolly, trans. *Didascalia Apostolorum* (Oxford: Clarendon Press, 1969), p. 147.

8. R. W. Church, trans. *St. Cyril of Jerusalem's Lectures on the Christian Sacraments* (London: S.P.C.K., 1960), p. 53.

9. T. Thompson, trans. *St. Ambrose "on the Mysteries" and the Treatise "on the Sacraments"* (London: S.P.C.K., 1919), pp. 98-99.

10. Paul W. Harkins, trans. *St. John Chrysostom: Baptismal Instructions* (Westminster: Newman Press, 1963), p. 53.

11. "Instructions to Candidates for Baptism," A. Mingana, trans., *Woodbrooke Studies* (Cambridge: Cambridge University Press, 1933), VI, 54.

12. John Wilkinson, trans. *Egeria's Travels* (London: S.P.C.K., 1971), pp. 144-46.

13. Cubié, Robert, *La lettre du pape Innocent Ier à Decentius de Gubbio* (Louvain: Publications Universitaires, 1973), p. 22.

14. "Enchiridion," Albert C. Outler, trans. *Augustine: Confessions and Enchiridion* (Philadelphia: Westminster Press, 1955), p. 366.

15. "Commentary on Psalm 64:10," *Patrologia Graeca*, XXIII, 640.

16. "Rule," Owen Chadwick, trans. *Western Asceticism* (Philadelphia: Westminster Press, 1958), p. 309.

17. "First Apology," Edward Rochie Hardy, trans. *Early Christian Fathers*, p. 287.

18. "Against the Heresies," Edward Rochie Hardy, trans. *Early Christian Fathers*, p. 388.

19. R. C. D. Jasper and G. J. Cuming, eds., *Prayers of the Eucharist*, third edition (Collegeville: Liturgical Press, 1987), p. 61. See this volume for texts of other early and reformed eucharistic prayers.

20. "The Genius of the Roman Rite," *Liturgica Historica* (Oxford: Clarendon Press, 1918), pp. 10, 19.

21. Darwell Stone, trans. *A History of the Doctrine of the Holy Eucharist* (London: Longmans, Green, and Co., 1909), I, 81.

22. Edward Rochie Hardy, trans. *Early Christian Fathers*, p. 287.

23. Cf. Thomas J. Talley, *The Origins of the Liturgical Year* (Collegeville: Liturgical Press, 1991), pp. 112–34.

24. John Wilkinson, trans. *Egeria's Travels* (London: S.P.C.K., 1971), p. 133.

25. Wilfrid Parson, trans. *Letter 55: to Januarius* (New York: Fathers of the Church, 1951), IX, 283.

26. "Life of Constantine," E. C. Richardson, trans. NPNF, 2nd series, I, 557.

27. John Wordsworth, trans. *Bishop Sarapion's Prayer-Book* (Hamden: Archon Books, 1964), p. 77.

28. Paul F. Bradshaw, *Ordination Rites of the Ancient Churches of East and West* (Collegeville: Liturgical Press, 1990), p. 116.

29. Ibid., p. 138.

30. Grant Sperry-White, *The Testamentum Domini: A Text for Students* (Bramcote: Alcuin-Grow Liturgical Studies, 1991), pp. 43–44.

31. Wilkinson, trans. *Egeria's Travels*, p. 131.

32. "Confessions," Albert C. Outler, trans. *Augustine: Confessions and Enchiridion* , p. 231.

Chapter III

1. Quoted in J. D. C. Fisher, *Christian Initiation: Baptism in the Medieval West: A Study in the Disintegration of the Primitive Rite of Initiation* (London: S.P.C.K., 1965), p. 137. Our approach follows Fisher.

2. J. G. Davies, *The Architectural Setting of Baptism* (London: Barrie and Rockliff, 1962), p. 69.

3. Trans. from *Enchiridion Symbolorum Definitionum et Declarationum*, ed. by Henry Denzinger and Adolf Schönmetzer, 33rd edition. (Freiburg: Herder, 1965), p. 333.

4. Ibid., p. 334.

5. Robert Taft, *The Liturgy of the Hours in East and West* (Collegeville: Liturgical Press, 1986), p. 23. Our treatment of the eastern office follows Taft.

6. Pierre Salmon, *The Breviary through the Centuries* (Collegeville: Liturgical Press, 1962), p. 25.

7. Cyrille Vogel, *Medieval Liturgy: An Introduction to the Sources* (Washington: Pastoral Press, 1986), p. 87.

8. James A. Muller, ed., *The Letters of Stephen Gardiner* (New York: Macmillan, 1933), p. 355. Spelling modernized.

9. Margaret R. Miles, *Image as Insight* (Boston: Beacon Press, 1985), pp. 95–125.

10. George R. McCracken and Allen Cabaniss, trans. *Early Medieval Theology* (Philadelphia: Westminster Press, 1957), pp. 90–147.

11. Eugene R. Fairweather, trans. "Why God Became Man," *A Scholastic Miscellany: Anselm to Ockham* (Philadelphia: Westminster Press, 1956), p. 134.

12. John T. McNeill and Helena M. Gamer, trans. *Medieval Handbooks of Penance* (New York: Columbia University Press, 1938), p. 88.

13. Elizabeth Frances Rogers, trans. *Peter Lombard and the Sacramental System* (Merrick, N.Y.: Richwood Publishing Co., 1976), p. 158.

14. Ibid., p. 171.

15. Fathers of the English Dominican Province, trans. *Summa Theologica* (New York: Benziger Brothers, 1948), III, 2672.

16. *Manual of York Use* manuscript, University Library, Cambridge, p. 23B.

17. William J. Irons and Isaac Williams, trans. *The Hymnal, 1940* (New York: Church Pension Fund, 1940), # 468.

18. Rogers trans., p. 233.

19. Yngve Brilioth, *A Brief History of Preaching* (Philadelphia: Fortress Press, 1965), p. 92.

20. For examples see Ray C. Petry, *No Uncertain Sound* (Philadelphia: Westminster Press, 1948) and Ray C. Petry, *Preaching in the Great Tradition* (Philadelphia: Westminster Press, 1950).

21. J. G. Davies, *The Secular Use of Church Buildings* (London: S.C.M., 1968).

22. Erwin Panofsky, trans. *Abbot Suger on the Abbey Church of St.-Denis and Its Treasures* 2nd ed. (Princeton: Princeton University Press, 1979), pp. 47, 49.

Chapter IV

1. "Concerning the Order of Public Worship," Paul Zeller Strodach and Ulrich S. Leupold, trans. *Luther's Works* (Philadelphia: Fortress Press, 1965), LIII, 11.

2. *Rituale Romanum* (Bassani: Remondini, 1834), p. 20.

3. "The Holy and Blessed Sacrament of Baptism," Charles M. Jacobs and E. Theodore Bachmann, trans. *Luther's Works* (Philadelphia: Muhlenberg Press: 1960), XXXV, 29.

4. *A Rational Illustration of the Book of Common Prayer* (London: Bohn, 1852), pp. 350–51.

5. *An Apology for The True Christian Divinity* (Manchester: William Irwin, 1869), pp. 257, 278.

6. "Draft Ecclesiastical Ordinances 1541," in K. S. Reid, trans. *Calvin: Theological Treatises* (Philadelphia: Westminster Press, 1954), p. 66.

7. "Canons and Dogmatic Decrees of the Council of Trent," in Philip Schaff, trans. *The Creeds of Christendom* (Grand Rapids: Baker Book House, n.d.), II, 125–26.

8. "Institutes," in Ford Lewis Battles, trans. *Calvin: Institutes of the Christian Religion* (Philadelphia: Westminster Press, 1960), II, 1461.

9. "A Form for Water Baptism," in H. Wayne Pipkin and John H. Yoder trans., *Balthasar Hubmaier, Theologian of Anabaptism* (Scottdale: Herald Press, 1989), p. 389.

10. "Foundation of Christian Doctrine," in John Christian Wenger, trans. *The Complete Writings of Menno Simons* (Scottdale: Herald Press, 1956) pp. 126–27.

11. "A Brief Apology," in Rollin Stely Armour, trans. *Anabaptist Baptism* (Scottdale: Herald Press, 1966), p. 53.

12. "Babylonian Captivity," in A. T. W. Steinhauser, Frederick C. Ahrens, and Abdel Ross Wentz, trans. *Luther's Works* (Philadelphia: Muhlenberg Press, 1959), XXXVI, 57.

13. Ibid., p. 69.

14. *Institutes*, II, 1303.

15. *The First and Second Prayer Books of Edward VI* (London: J. M. Dent & Sons, 1949), p. 236.

16. Barclay, *An Apology for the True Christian Divinity* (Manchester: William Irwin, 1869), p. 215.

17. Ibid., p. 257.

18. Ibid., p. 240.

19. Robert Taft, *The Liturgy of the Hours in East and West* (Washington: Pastoral Press, 1986), p. 302.

20. Hughes Oliphant Old, "Daily Prayer in the Reformed Church of Strasbourg, 1525–1530," *Worship*, LII (1978), 121–38.

21. "The German Mass," in Augustus Steimle and Ulrich S. Leupold, trans. *Luther's Works* (Philadelphia: Fortress Press, 1965) LIII, 68.

22. *First and Second Prayer Books*, p. 3.

23. Diane Karay Tripp, "Daily Prayer in the Reformed Tradition: an Initial Survey," *Studia Liturgica*, XXI, 76-107, 190-219.

24. *The Confession of Faith* (Philadelphia: Towar and Hogan, 1829), pp. 595-96.

25. Jerome Theisen, *Mass Liturgy and the Council of Trent* (Collegeville: St. John's University Press, 1965).

26. I. Pahl, ed., *Coena Domini I* (Freiburg: Universitätsverlag, 1983).

27. Günther Stiller, *Johann Sebastian Bach and Liturgical Life in Leipzig* (St. Louis: Concordia Press, 1984), p. 49.

28. *Institutes*, II, 1421.

29. Horton Davies, *The Worship of the American Puritans, 1629–1730* (New York: Peter Lang, 1990), p. 163.

30. Paul Meyendorff, "The Liturgical Reforms of Nikon" (Unpublished Ph.D. dissertation, University of Notre Dame, 1986).

31. Piet Schoonenberg, "Transubstantiation: How Far is This Doctrine Historically Determined?" in *The Sacraments: An Ecumenical Dilemma* (New York: Paulist Press, 1966), pp. 78–91.

32. *Institutes*, II, 1370.

33. Francis Clark, *Eucharistic Sacrifice and the Reformation*, 2nd edition (Oxford: Blackwell, 1967).

34. Leigh Eric Schmidt, *Holy Fairs: Scottish Communions and American Revivals* (Princeton: Princeton University Press, 1989).

35. *The Mass of the Roman Rite* (New York: Benziger Brothers, 1951), I, 142.

36. "Formula Missae," Paul Zeller Strodach and Ulrich S. Lupold, trans. *Luther's Works*, LIII, 23.

37. "The Book of Discipline," in *John Knox's History of the Reformation in Scotland* (London: Thomas Nelson and Sons, 1949), II, 281.

38. *The Westminster Directory* (Bramcote: Grove Books, 1980), 23.

39. Ibid., p. 24.

40. Ibid., p. 32.

41. Trent, Schaff, II, 151.

42. Beverley Nitschke, "The Third Sacrament? Confession and Forgiveness in the *Lutheran Book of Worship*" (Unpublished Ph.D. dissertation, University of Notre Dame, 1988).

43. *Commentary on True and False Religion* (Durham: Labyrinth Press, 1981), pp. 255–56.

44. *Institutes*, II, 1468.

45. *The Canons and Decrees of the Council of Trent*, H. J. Schroeder, trans. (Rockford: Tan books, 1978), p. 185.

46. Trent, Schaff, II, 187.

47. Paul F. Bradshaw, *The Anglican Ordinal* (London: S.P.C.K., 1971), p. 24.

48. "To the Christian Nobility of the German Nation," Charles M. Jacobs and James Atkinson, trans. *Luther's Works*, XLIV, 128–29.

49. "The Ordination of Ministers of the Word," *Luther's Works*, LIII, 124–26.

50. *Institutes*, II, 1476.

51. "Draft Ecclesiastical Ordinances, 1541", K. S. Reid trans. *Calvin: Theological Treatises*, (Philadelphia: Westminster Press, 1954), p. 58.

52. *American Puritans*, p. 223.

53. Yngve Brilioth, *A Brief History of Preaching* (Philadelphia: Fortress Press, 1965), p. 118.

54. Ibid., p. 162.

55. Charles Garside, Jr., *Zwingli and the Arts* (New Haven: Yale University Press, 1966), pp. 6–26.

56. Friedrich Blume, et al., *Protestant Church Music* (London: Victor Gollancz, 1975), p. 510.

57. James F. White, *Protestant Worship and Church Architecture* (New York: Oxford University Press, 1964).

58. Rudolf Wittkower and Irma B. Jaffe, editors, *Baroque Art: The Jesuit Contribution* (New York: Fordham University Press, 1972).

59. Nigel Yates, *Buildings, Faith and Worship* (Oxford: Clarendon Press, 1991), p. 77.

Chapter V

1. Immanuel Kant, *Religion Within the Limits of Reason Alone*, Theodore M. Greene and Hoyt H. Hudson, trans. (New York: Harper & Row, 1960), p. 182.

2. Ibid., p. 188.

3. *A Short History of the Western Liturgy*, 2nd ed. (Oxford: Oxford University Press, 1979), pp. 117–52.

4. *The Teaching of the Church Regarding Baptism*, Ernest A. Payne, trans. (London: S.C.M. Press, 1948), from a lecture given in 1943.

5. (Vatican City: Vatican Polyglot Press, 1980).

6. John C. S. Nias, *Gorham and the Bishop of Exeter* (London: S.P.C.K., 1951).

7. *The Rites* (New York: Pueblo Publishing Company, 1988), IA, 48–169.

8. (Geneva: World Council of Churches, 1982), p. 6.

9. George Guiver, *Company of Voices* (New York: Pueblo Press, 1988), pp. 137–39.

10. *Constitution on the Sacred Liturgy* (Collegeville: Liturgical Press, 1963), p. 51.

11. *The Liturgy of the Hours in East and West* (Collegeville: Liturgical Press, 1986), pp. 314–15.

12. "The Rules of the United Societies," in Albert C. Outler, ed., *John Wesley* (New York: Oxford University Press, 1964), p. 178.

13. *Lectures on Revivals of Religion*, William G. McLoughlin, ed. (Cambridge: Harvard University Press, 1960), p. 259.

14. (Dayton: W. R. Funk, 1900).

15. Enrico Cattaneo, *Il Culto Cristiano in Occidente*, 2nd ed. (Rome: Edizioni Liturgiche, 1984), pp. 435–51.

16. (Benjamin Hoadly), *A Plain Account of the Nature and End of the Sacrament of the Lord's-Supper*, 2nd ed. (London: James, John, and Paul Kanoptan, 1735), p. 24.

17. *The Eucharistic Hymns of John and Charles Wesley*, J. Ernest Rattenbury, ed. (Cleveland: O.S.L. Publications, 1991).

18. *The Christian System* (New York: Arno Press and New York Times, 1969), p. 325.

19. (Cincinnati: L. Swormstedt & J. T. Mitchell, 1844), p. 78.

20. *Camp Meeting Manual, A Practical Book for the Camp Ground* (Boston: H. V. Degen, 1855), p. 18.

21. Finney, *Lectures on Revivals*, p. 250.

22. "On Borrowed Time: The Christian Year in American Methodism, 1784–1960," (unpublished Ph.D. dissertation, Drew University, 1991), pp. 123, 163–69.

23. Fred Winslow Adams, *The Christian Year*. 2nd ed. (New York: Federal Council of Churches, 1940), p. 4.

24. Outler, *John Wesley*, p. 181.

25. *The Rites* (New York: Pueblo Publishing Company, 1976), 1:337–445.

26. p. 41.

27. Karen Westerfield-Tucker, "'Till Death Us Do Part'" (unpublished Ph.D. dissertation, University of Notre Dame, 1992).

28. (Philadelphia: Fortress Press, 1987).

29. (Chicago: Liturgy Training Publications, 1989).

30. *John Wesley's Prayer Book: The Sunday Service of the Methodists in North America*, James F. White, ed. (Cleveland: O.S.L. Publications, 1991).

31. *Apostolicae Curae*, September 13, 1896.

32. (Geneva: World Council of Churches, 1982).

33. Leonardo Boff, *Ecclesiogenesis: The Base Communities Reinvent the Church* (Maryknoll: Orbis Books, 1986), p. 25.

34. David Stoll, *Is Latin America Turning Protestant?* (Berkeley: University of California Press, 1990).

35. Horton Davies, *Worship and Theology in England* (Princeton: Princeton University Press, 1961), III, 143.

36. Jay P. Dolan, *Catholic Revivalism* (Notre Dame: University of Notre Dame Press, 1978), p. 89.

37. "Tra le sollecitudini," *The New Liturgy*, Kevin Seasoltz, ed. (New York: Herder & Herder, 1966), pp. 3–10.

38. Michael W. Harris, *The Rise of Gospel Blues* (New York: Oxford University Press, 1992).

39. James F. White, *Protestant Worship and Church Architecture* (New York: Oxford University Press, 1964), pp. 98–105.

40. James F. White, *The Cambridge Movement: The Ecclesiologists and the Gothic Revival* (Cambridge: Cambridge University Press, 1962).

Chapter VI

1. (Collegeville: Liturgical Press, 1963), p. 17.

2. (Geneva: World Council of Churches, 1982).

INDEX

SUBJECTS